An introduction to the workings of the Internet for Small Businesses

Mike Sussex

Cover design by Rob Miller

Contents

Chapter 1: What this book is all about

Introduction

The Internet has been around in pretty much its current form since the early 1990s, back then it was a mostly obscure niche plaything enjoyed by people who preferred speaking Klingon to each other and engaging in heated debates as to whether Captain Kirk was the only true captain of the USS Enterprise or had Jean-Luc Picard made it his own. Fortunately, (if not at least for the hairstyles of the time), the 1990s are now a distant memory, but the Internet has grown up considerably from those times. Yes, there are still arguments conducted in Klingon about all things Star Trek related, but nowadays the Internet (or web) has a far broader reach, people now for instance can (and do) spend hours on video sites like YouTube watching cats be wheeled around the room on automatic vacuum cleaners. Ah, progress!

On a more serious note however, the Internet has become in the intervening 25+ years, a place where people not only communicate, but transact business. Millions of companies have a presence on the Internet transacting billions of dollars of business on a monthly basis, from the behemoths (the names of which we are all too familiar with: Microsoft, Google, Apple, eBay, Amazon, the list is comprehensive), to the one-man band company operating out of a rented office in downtown Anytown, completing a couple of orders a week online, everyone is doing it. The question is how? How do these people manage to achieve this feat, they can't all be computer scientists with nothing better to do with their time? To the uninitiated, the Internet may as well be magic – most people have no idea how it works, all they know is that they search for something and Google finds it, and if they want to watch a video then YouTube has it. And they can be quite content with that level of knowledge; the difference here is that you are a small business owner or manager, you are conducting business to some extent online, and if that revenue stream stops for whatever reason, your nerves are going to take even more of a hit than they do on a daily basis because you now have another problem to deal with, and with this one being related to the Internet, and it being magic, then you had better get to finding your wand pretty quickly!

While I cannot say that this book is the magic wand that you will be looking for in your hour of need, it can at least go some way to explaining - like the magic tricks of Penn and Teller and David Copperfield - it's not really magic (sorry if that has spoiled something for you), but with the correct knowledge, you can understand what is happening rather than being misdirected. This book is a high-level overview of the very basics that every small business owner or manager should know, so that informed and intelligent decisions relating to an Internet presence can be maintained without becoming lost in the mess of jargon and phrases and sometimes misinformation that is so easily gotten into when coming at this for the first time. This book can also serve as a high-level refresher for those of you who have been through the process before and just need to remind yourself of some topics.

And here you are, the proud owner of a book to make it all better and make the Internet suddenly completely understandable. While I can't promise that, I can say that if you are reading this for the first time, then by following through each chapter in sequence, you'll find that they build on the knowledge gained in the last, and by the end you'll at least be less daunted by the words and phrases and the "magic". Many will find that they will go through this book a couple of times, and that's fine, it is arranged in a way that you can jump in and out as required, so please, if that is your preference, use the book as a reference as opposed to a fixed beginning to end recipe. Jump around the chapters as you see fit, that works just fine too. Enjoy.

Why target small businesses?

So why then is this book aimed squarely at the small business owner/manager, rather than a more generic audience? Well, there is nothing to say that a more generic audience would not benefit from it, but experience shows that in the setting of a small business it is often the case that there really are too few people to be able to accomplish all of the tasks required, and quite often tasks such as the website and e-mail and so on are farmed out to "the IT guy", or some consultancy company or whatever the solution is. And this is absolutely fine at the outset, but IT people come and go, relationships with consultancies come and go, and sooner or later something needs to be dealt with. Everyone who set it up has moved on or their services are no longer used, the problem lands on the desk of the manager or owner – because let's face it, in a small business, all of the curly problems end up there because you are supposed to know everything - with a solution expected whilst other people around the place are quite quickly falling into panic mode.

To be in that situation with absolutely no knowledge of where you are, nor an obvious (and not hugely expensive) way out is not ideal, and it is certainly not the time that you need to be cramming to obtain the knowledge that you need in order to move forward.

This book is not about delving into the very depths of exactly how the Internet works (although we will cover a little bit about it), you're not going to find yourself having to learn program code and you're not going to need to learn the model and serial numbers of loads of different components; instead, it will give you the grounding to understand that if a problem occurs, and the world is falling apart for your business at a spectacular rate, that you will at least be able to narrow down the possible causes of the problem and know where to look for a solution which will save you valuable time and money. Besides, it's just good stuff to know anyway.

The role of an 'IT guy'

Most of us know the IT guy: if you don't then you can quite often recognise them from some distance, mostly by the neckbeard, the geekily funny maths-related t-shirt, and the faint but lingering smell of pizza and coffee which seems to follow them around.

Despite the stereotypical image of your friendly geek there, they are very useful people to know as they do tend to know a reasonable amount of stuff about all sorts of things. Most IT people you meet (if they ever come out of their house that is) will tell you that because they "work with computers" that they end up becoming responsible for, and garner a wealth of knowledge upon, everything that has a plug attached to it. This is not by choice on their part but the nature of your typical IT guy is that they learn new skills at a pretty decent rate, and will not be beaten by a problem. Hence, the random broken thing with a plug arrives, and rather than give it back, will learn why the thing is broken, and how to fix it.

Why does all this matter though, amusing as it is? Well, if you have your IT guy already, then what is the betting that everything that comes up – either with a plug or just techie related – will be handballed to that person without a second thought? It's almost always the case, and for the IT guy that's a great result: they are getting to learn about something new and you are paying them for it. Who could ask for more?

This is absolutely in no way a bad thing, having someone on the team that knows everything techie about your business and is willing to learn what they don't already know is an enviable situation for most businesses, and they are a quality asset. Whilst they are there. And that's where the problem starts: when your IT guy goes – and they will, eventually. IT guys tend to move around a bit and when they do, your training and the sum of your businesses techie knowledge walks out the door too.

Now you are back to zero. Well, not exactly zero, it's a bit worse than that in reality. Before your IT guy left, you had the conversation that went something like:

You: *"Be sure you note down absolutely everything we need to know before you go"*

And that's exactly what happened. Now you are staring at either a dog-eared, coffee-stained single side of A4 replete with seemingly random letters, numbers, symbols and phrases as well as assorted scrawled notes or, you have a tome the size of War and Peace that you've dragged out of the cupboard and dusted off which, in order to be understood, requires a degree in computer science just to get past the title.

And that's the time you realise that having a general understanding of the way in which the Internet works might be a decent bit of knowledge to have.

What you need to know, and what you don't

As a small business owner or manager, the knowledge you are going to need falls somewhere between "It's all made of magic" and being able to write a thesis on packet switching (of which, more later but fear not). You need to know enough to understand what the cryptic side of A4 notes might mean and where we might head in order to apply them, but not so much we get bogged down in the intricacies of every part of the Internet such that we never see the light of day again.

This book will get you to that stage: enough not to be confused by the technical bits, but not deep enough to be scary to the uninitiated.

A little bit of knowledge ...

While it is the aim of this book to move you off of square one, we need to be careful. Knowing a little bit is very useful and can absolutely get you out of trouble and heading in the right direction, but this book is not the Internet start to finish, it will not teach you everything and isn't designed to try. If your business world is falling apart by the minute or you are in the process of making big decisions for the future of the company you will still very likely be short of knowledge in key areas, and those situations are not the times to be running out of knowledge. You are more than likely still going to need professional assistance but at least when that outside assistance is consulted or employed, you will be able to communicate in a sensible manner and understand what each other wants and needs.

Chapter 2: An Internet of pieces

The big picture: what are all of the puzzle pieces

Let's get started with diving into the meat of the problem then. The first thing that we are going to address is that the Internet as a system may at the outset appear to be this big, scary, complex beast of a thing (and to some degree that is true) but the trick to understanding it - like understanding any system of size - is to break it down into manageable and easily understandable pieces. That's what we are going to do here, and the chapters that begin here and continue to the end of the book will each address one of those pieces.

Where we actually have a bit of good fortune is that with the Internet each of the individual pieces is easily thought of on its own, and it's quite easy to see how they fit together once they are understood more clearly.

The overall puzzle

The Internet at its core is a system by which data is passed back and forth between computers, most people would see that data expressed as a webpage or as an image or a video. It is actually a little bit more complex than that but fortunately not too much more. Let's start with discussing the nature of that data in very simple terms: when you look at a webpage for example, your web browser sends a request to "the Internet", and it, in return (hopefully) shows the website that you are interested in. On the face of it that is quite a simple sounding problem to solve, but there are a fair number of pieces involved there: how do we know where to find the web page in the first instance, how do we get all the bits of that web page from where it resides to the computer or device that we are using, how do we know that the data we are passing back is an image of a cat and not some scrambled text? How did the producer of the website put it there in the first place and make it available for us to find? All of these questions and a bunch more will be answered as we go through the various chapters contained in the book; we will look at the pieces of the puzzle that allow the various servers, routers, switches and other equipment along the way, to send that image of a cat back to your computer from the other side of the world, on demand, (almost) every single time.

In a minute we are going to look at how we go about getting our favourite web page to be shown on the device that we are using, but beforehand, I will introduce the first bit of terminology which will come up time and again in the remainder of the text. For the vast majority of you there will be sighs of exasperation and slapping of foreheads, but the nature of this book is to try to teach these things from the very beginning, so please bear with me here as not everyone knows this. The term is *web browser*, and for the avoidance of doubt, the definition of a web browser is as follows:

A web browser is a software program that is placed upon the device being used with the specific purpose of navigating around the Internet. It achieves this via the sending and receiving of data in response to a request, and organising the resultant response so as to display that response in a manner that the designer of the web page had intended on the device in use. There are hundreds of web browsers available but for the most part there are a few leading contenders as below (shown with their corresponding logos which were correct at the time of publishing):

"Chrome" published by Google Inc.

"Internet Explorer published by Microsoft Corp.

"Firefox" published by Mozilla Foundation.

"Edge" published by Microsoft Corp.

"Safari" published by Apple Corp.

"Opera" published by Opera Software ASA.

Table 1: Web browsers in use at time of publishing

We'll begin here at a very high level, and we will address the issue of how does our web browser handle the communications required in order to display the web page of interest. One of the easiest ways to think about how this process works is to compare it to the telephone network; they are in fact really quite similar.

Let us assume that you are looking to put your car in for a service at the local dealership, and look at the steps involved as to how you might do that over the phone:

1. You're going to ascertain the name of the dealership that you would like to contact
2. You're going to look their number up in the phone book
3. You're going to call their number – the phone company will route the call for you, we don't really care how they do that, as long as they do it properly
4. When you reach the company concerned, you're going to request the servicing department and the receptionist will route your call – again, we don't care how that happens
5. And finally, you're going to book the service and hang up

All seems pretty straightforward actually, but each of those steps relates almost directly to the steps involved in making a request for the web page over the Internet, let's look at how they might align:

1. To ascertain the name of the website we want to look for, we are going to enter their *Domain Name*
2. Your web browser will consult the publicly available *Name Servers* to see where the web site resides - we don't care how it does that, just as long as it does, and reports it back to your web browser
3. Your web browser goes where the name servers tell it, and the entries found there – known as *DNS (Domain Name System)* records – tell your web browser how to route the request to the correct location – we don't really care how, as long as it does it properly

4. Your web browser routes its request for your website as it is instructed to do, again, we don't care how, just that it does, and finally (hopefully),
5. The server hosting the web page that we were looking for sends back the data to your web browser and the request is completed and terminated.

As you can see, the steps are basically the same, it's just the terminology in the middle that is different.

Using this very simple analogy is in fact going to be incredibly helpful for you as we go through in a bit more detail what each of these pieces of the puzzle are, so try to keep it in mind. And perhaps if you get to a point later in the book where things don't seem as clear as you might like, maybe come back to this analogy to see where it might fit in, as it may help.

With the above analogy fresh in our minds, we are going to jump into deconstructing each part of it, but in what at first may seem like an odd move, we are going to start not at the beginning of step one, but just a little after it at step 2. Bear with me on this, as I shall explain: when calling your local dealership to make the appointment, we already know the name of the dealership to use, if not their phone number, so before we get to dial the number we are first of all going to look for their phone number in the phone book. All pretty straightforward and easy of course, but it rather glosses over the fact that in order to have a listing in the phone book the dealership must first have a phone number. The same is true when dealing with navigating to web pages: our analogous steps nonchalantly went with "enter their domain name" but computers don't really deal in words, they deal in numbers, so before we can get a domain name (our entry in the phone book) we must first have a number to associate it with. That number, is known as an *IP address* and is the most fundamental underpinning of the Internet.

So, with that in mind, let's look at the numbers we need to know about.

Chapter 3: IP Addresses

IP Addresses: The keys to the kingdom

As people, we see the world as words: it doesn't matter what language we speak, they are mostly made up of words. For us in everyday life words are incredibly useful, they allow us to express our innermost thoughts and complex ideas. Some of them have even been used to write a book on how the Internet works!

That's all great, but words have a downside too, they are not only complex but they often have multiple meanings, there are many words that mean the same thing, and the same word used in a different context can completely change its meaning and importance. Not to mention that each language has its own words and its own meanings and interpretations for any number of words. For a computer, and by extension a network of computers (which the Internet is: in the early days of the Internet it was known by some as "a network of networks"), words therefore are far too random; computers instead – as you probably already know – deal in numbers, specifically, they deal in binary numbers being as there are only two possibilities – 1 and 0 (true and false). Binary numbers offer a huge advantage to a computer in that they are limitless (unlike words), they are unique – there is only ever one of every number regardless of how large or small that number is - and they can be added together very easily and quickly; after all, a computer is little more than a glorified calculator.

There are a couple of downsides to counting in binary though: namely that we as people are easily confused and for the most part cannot read them easily, so we wouldn't immediately know that *1001101* for instance is equal to 77, and secondly as we can see, it is a relatively long way of handling numbers taking 7 characters there to achieve what we achieve in two, and that problem only gets worse when dealing with large numbers. To combat this, although the computer deals internally in binary, it gives us a little bit of a break and shows us the base-10 (decimal) numbers that we are used to seeing. After all, it is people like us that have to interact with these computers and make them work, so they can cut us a little slack from time to time.

So why all this talk of binary and decimal numbers?

When we have a network of computers, or for that matter, a number of anything, using words to describe them quickly becomes either too lengthy to be of practical use, or we actually run out of words that we can use to adequately cover all of the possibilities because ‘device A’ is not sufficiently different to ‘device B’ as to be identifiable: think what happens when you have purchased a few laptops at the same time for your company: they are all the same make and model, they are all the same size and colour and everything else. Usually, they are identical in every way. In small companies, people often get around this by sticking a sticker on the laptop with “John’s laptop” written on it. Of course, when John leaves and Jane takes his place, either Jane keeps a laptop with someone else’s name on it, or we get a new sticker. A fair and reasonable solution for a small company, but when you are dealing with anything more than a couple of dozen devices, the practicalities of the solution break down very quickly. Even medium sized companies would normally have a couple of hundred devices, a multi-national might have twenty thousand or so. Great for the makers of stickers, but not great for the person having to go around and stick them all on.

We need a better solution if we are to identify the tens of millions of devices that we need to reference on the Internet; we know that our sticker plan is a complete non-starter, and so too any notion of referring to these machines by some kind of description – this would be especially problematic when we consider that those descriptions would need to span every language in the world.

So, we are left with having to identify the devices on the Internet using numbers, it is the only logical way because numbers are infinitely scalable there is no realistic maximum value. The natural choice for a computer network here therefore, would be to identify all of these devices using a binary number seeing as that's how they would identify themselves anyway, but as mentioned earlier, binary isn't particularly space efficient so you could imagine the size of the label required for numbers over about a million, not to mention that as people, our eyes would get all confused with the long strings of ones and zeros and all sorts of trouble could result.

What is left therefore, is to use decimal numbers. And the chosen solution to the problem was a specific arrangement of decimal numbers called an *IP Address*.

IP addresses are a very sensible compromise; they combine the scalability of using numbers while not getting into the trap of huge strings of numbers that people are not good at dealing with. There are in fact two different types of IP address for reasons that we will get onto in a bit, but for the purposes of this book, we will deal with what is known as IPv4: named because it was the fourth version of the *Internet Protocol*. The other type of IP address that you will come across is IPv6 - no prizes for guessing that it is the sixth generation of the Internet Protocol. At the time of writing however (2016), IPv6 is not really in common usage although that will change over time for reasons we will get onto in just a moment. For now though we'll deal with IPv4 addresses as you will see them quite frequently as you get an understanding of how the Internet works; and they become fundamental when we talk about *DNS* a little later in the book.

We'll start with what an IPv4 address (which from here on will just be referred to as IP address) actually looks like, then we'll take a bit of a dive into how it is constructed before we look at how they are used and obtained and so on.

An IP address is made up of four, three-digit number groups – known as *octets* - separated by a dot (or a period if you prefer), which is why the notation is sometimes referred to as a *dotted quad*. The numbers in each group can theoretically contain any of the numbers between 0 and 255, giving a maximum of 256 possibilities in each group.

Stepping aside for just a moment, let's look at the reason for those numbers that have just been quoted: 255 and 256. Why would they ever be chosen as the upper end of the range and the count of possible numbers when they seem so random? The clue comes when we take a look at the *binary* counting system – I am sure that most of you will know that binary is made up of 0s and 1s, and that's how a computer does all of its calculations. Everything comes down to 0s which represent "off" or "false" and 1s which mean "on" or "true". For a computer, each 0 or 1 is called a *bit*, being the smallest amount of information that it is able to store. Bits are grouped together in sets of eight to form *Bytes*. Bytes often represent what we would usually know as a character – a letter or number or punctuation symbol for example.

If we take a look at our eight bits (our byte) and put it into binary, we get any combination between 00000000 and 11111111. If you don't know already, whereas the human numbering system has units (on the right hand side of a number), tens to the left of it, hundreds to the left again – basically increasing by a factor of 10 each column, binary does the same but in twos. So, the rightmost digit still has a value of 1, but the digit to the left of it 2, then 4, 8, 16 and so on. With eight bits in our byte, and all of them set to a value of 1 (true), then we end up with the following sum:

1 + 2 + 4 + 8 + 16 + 32 + 64 + 128

They total 255, the additional number (the 256th value in our range) is 0, for when all eight bits are set to zero, false or off.

From our byte we derive *Kilobyte* (1000 bytes), *Megabyte* (1 million bytes) and *Gigabyte* (1 billion bytes) and so on.

What we have here in the case of our IP address is a four-byte number, more commonly though, it is called a 32-bit number (so called because with each byte being eight bits, we have four of them, so 4x8 = 32). 32-bit was the de facto standard of computer processing for decades, and only recently has it been overtaken by the more capacious 64-bit but that's a conversation very much for another time.

An example of an IPv4 IP address would be:

192.168.0.1 Or in a more longhand format, 192.168.000.001, both are the same and equally valid.

With 256 theoretical possible numbers in each octet (or byte), we can see how when the original creators of the IP address system invented it, they couldn't conceive of there being more devices that there were possible numbers. Remember though that the IP address system was originally conceived somewhere in the 1970s and computers were still very rare, and those that did exist were almost exclusively for use in universities and multi-national companies, and let's be honest, they were half the size of the average bedroom. With computers that size, it would be likely that we would run out of land area before running out of IP addresses.

So how many IPv4 addresses are there?

So far I have referred to theoretical maximum numbers and there is good reason for that. First of all, the theoretical maximum number of IPv4 addresses is 2^{32} or 4,294,967,296 – approximately 4.2 billion. The reason that it is theoretical is that not all of those numbers are available for use; they don't start at 0.0.0.0 and just keep being increased until they reach 255.255.255.255. For a start, there are no IP addresses that start with 0 in the first octet; everything starting with 10 in the first octet or 192 in the first octet is used for private addresses and are not reachable on the Internet. In all there are about 288 million addresses that cannot be used, it still leaves about 4 billion which is a decent number, but if you now think about how many websites there are available if you do a web search, they would account for a big chunk of that number. There are millions and millions of other addresses in use for Internet accessible addresses that are not websites too – we'll cover a few of these a little later, but by way of an example, think about VoIP phones, they all need an IP address, so too your web-enabled printer and other devices, all those security monitoring systems with webcams that can be seen online, all of the home users connected to the Internet around the world. Suddenly, with those sorts of numbers and even some fridges being connected to the Internet nowadays, our massive pool of 4 billion numbers is starting to look more like a pond than an ocean.

It was due to the rapidly shrinking nature of the IP address pool, that it was noticed a number of years ago that given the current rate of usage of addresses, they would run out in fairly short order. In fact, the allocation of the last IP address from the *Primary address pool* was made in February 2011. Now that's nothing to worry about at the moment because here we are five years later on and the world is still spinning, the web still works and there are more cat pictures and videos online than there ever has been. It will be a problem, but the solution is already being implemented. That solution is IPv6. Being the next public release of the Internet Protocol (don't ask what happened to v5) IPv6 dramatically increases the number of addresses that will be available to a point that just absolutely cannot be reached. Famous last words there of course, people said that about IPv4 and now look at the situation. That said, the day of reckoning for the complete exhaustion of IPv4 addresses is still some way off, so for now you really only need have a passing notion of the existence of IPv6 as it is not commonly in use yet. It will be though, and over the coming years it will play an ever greater role in the way the Internet works so it will be useful to have a basic understanding of it and how it works.

IPv6 addresses abandon the dotted quad notation of addressing. In fact, they abandon the idea of a decimal numbering system entirely, opting instead for what is called *Hexadecimal notation* – that is being able to count to 16 in a single digit (being 0-9 as normal, followed by A = 10, B = 11 and so on until F = 15). So now with each number going to 15 instead of the usual 9, there being more blocks – up from four to eight - and more numbers in each block (up from three to four), the change and the effect is profound. Not only in terms of the number of available addresses, but in the way that they are written.

With IPv6 there will be 2^{128} addresses available, when changed into numbers that we understand, it is 3,403 $x10^{35}$ that's 3403 with 36 zeros after it. There is probably a name for that number but I don't know what it is. It's bloody big though. It looks like this: 3,403,000,000,000,000,000,000,000,000,000,000,000,000

We're not going to spend much time looking at IPv6 because at the moment it really isn't that prevalent and at least for the time being you are unlikely to encounter them very often. What

I will do though is show you want an IPv6 address looks like just so that they won't come completely out of left field if you do bump into one.

As I mentioned, they are written in eight blocks of four hexadecimal numbers, so look like this:

2001:0DB8:AC10:FE01:0000:0000:0000:0000

There are variants to this because blocks of all zeros can be omitted, so the same could be written as:

2001:0DB8:AC10:FE01::

Notice the double colon at the end to signify default (missing) blocks.

They are far more complicated but the notation of them still makes it possible for our simple human brains to comprehend and read if required.

That's where we are going to leave the IPv6 discussion for now because to start delving any deeper rather goes beyond the scope of this book. In fact, that's where we are going to leave the description of all IP addresses, and move on from what they are and how they work to what you can do with them and how you can get your hands on them.

Do I need one, do I need more, how do I get them?

You've probably worked out already that if you want some kind of presence on the Internet – be that a website, some e-mail or even a connection from your home or office to the Internet – then yes, you are going to need an IP address. Some people need more than one, some people need hundreds of them; you can rest assured though that if you are reading this book then you are probably only going to need one, the question then becomes less *"Do I need one"* and more *"How do I get mine?"*

All IP addresses are regulated by a central organisation called the Internet Assigned Numbers Authority (IANA), and they in turn allocate blocks of IP addresses to region-based Regional Internet Registries (RIRs) - there are five of them:

AFRINIC – which handles IP addresses for Africa,

APNIC – for the Asia/Pacific,

ARIN – North America mostly,

LACNIC – Latin America mostly, and

RIPE NCC – which deals with Europe, Middle East and Central Asia

These regional registries then distribute the IP addresses allocated to them, out to companies, which would normally be *Internet Service Providers (ISPs)* which are the companies from which you purchase your connection to the Internet, or to independent hosting companies and some large businesses. You, in turn would get your IP address from one of these entities, almost always though your IP address will come from your ISP or your hosting company.

Generally speaking, if you are getting an IP address from your ISP – which would normally be the case for your office connection to the Internet, you would have a single IP address which would identify your company on the network, and this is fine because for the most part people will not need to find the address of your company; your connection to the Internet would be used (almost always) exclusively for looking outward to the Internet as opposed to others on the Internet looking inward to your business. The reason for this is that you would normally not – at least in a small business environment – be hosting your own website, e-mail or other web-based services in-house, you would use a hosting company for those tasks. We are going to look at hosting companies, the services they provide and how they provide them in later chapters.

The takeaway from this chapter is that every device on the Internet needs to be identified, and it is identified by its IP address, that address comes from a pool of known numbers and is allocated to you by an entity with which you probably already have some kind of dealing.

Chapter 4: Getting from A to B

As has been mentioned in the previous chapter, all Internet-connected devices are identified by an IP address which has been assigned to that device (usually) by our ISP or, if we are a bigger company, by the Regional Internet Registry (RIR), and that's all great but there are billions of IP addresses in use and they are spread around every part of the globe, so how – literally, on Earth – do we know that a given IP address resides on a server in a rack of a data centre somewhere on the outskirts of Sydney in Australia, and not actually a PC under someone's desk in Los Angeles, California for example?

To answer this rather fundamental question we are going to take a little look at the concept of routing – essentially, knowing where a given IP address is supposed to be pointed towards. I will be the first to confess that this is by no means at all necessary to know when getting to know how the Internet works, and if it is not something that you are particularly interested in, please feel free to skip to the next chapter, I won't be offended, I promise. If you were to skip to the next chapter then you will find that we talk about domain names ... finally, a word that you may have already encountered on your travels, as opposed to all these new ones. Of course you'll still get that pay off if you stick around and follow through with this chapter, but when you get there, you'll know just that little bit more about the underpinnings of the Internet, and that can only be a good thing.

The subject of routing of IP addresses is a massively deep and complicated subject, one that if explored fully not only goes well beyond the scope of this book, but one that would leave your average computer science graduate with a physically spinning head. Therefore, we are not going to explore it in anywhere near that amount of detail here; what we are going to do is just look at the basics of how the Internet knows which server your website of interest lives on, and how it might know where to look in order to find that priceless video of a cat riding around the kitchen on a robotic vacuum cleaner; we all know that's what people really use the Internet to find after all.

Before we get into the specifics and ins and outs of the process, we are going to introduce a potentially new word to your vocabulary: *Router*. There are no prizes for guessing the purpose of such a device but we'll peel back the covers a little bit and see how it does what it does.

Without probably even knowing it, you already have a router and use it every day; for most people their experience of a router will start and end with the modem that connects to the Internet via the telephone socket – this is especially true in a home office environment. If you take a second to look at that box – whether it is one that was supplied to you by your ISP or one that your IT guy installed for you – for the most part, you'll see that it has a number of sockets (or *ports*) on it: one of which will head off to the wall socket and the others – of which there are often four and usually coloured yellow – will usually be empty but if they are not, they will be connected to various PCs and other devices around about the place. In an office environment these routers will usually be bigger with eight, sixteen or more "yellow" ports on them. It doesn't actually matter how many ports the device has, its purpose is the same.

That router has at least two *Interfaces*: one will be marked as the internal (or local) interface, the others will be referred to as external. And it is this distinction that is the key to how a router, and by extension, the Internet works. The job of the router is to know how to direct the "traffic" of requests – it will either route them to the internal interface, in which case the request will end up going to one of the devices connected to the yellow ports, or it will direct the request through one of the external interfaces so that another router along the chain can deal with the request that this router cannot answer for itself. This process is repeated for router after router in the chain until we find the item we are looking for – in this case, our Roomba cat.

Let's then look at how this might work in the real world for us: we'll imagine for the sake of this analogy that we need to visit a client who works on the other side of the world to us. We have their company name and their address, and we have to get there so that we can get the all-important contract signed. How might we go about getting from where we are to where we need to be? We will start by arriving in the right country (preferably at the airport or dock that is closest to the town or city in which our client works), we will then head in the general direction of your destination based upon any large town or city that may be close to our final destination. As we start to get closer to that major town the direction signs dotted along the route start to become more specific – instead of maybe giving the names of only major towns and cities that we are heading in the direction of, they start to list the smaller towns along the route. Eventually we reach the town that we are visiting, from there, the number of roads available to you is limited, and a local resource (like the friendly post office or pub staff) can point to the street that you are after. Once we are on the right street all we need to do is to get to the correct number along the street and we have arrived at our destination. From the other side of the world, we have been zeroing in on this one place using the signs available to us which become increasingly precise until we arrived.

Using our series of routers around the Internet we do things in much the same sort of way.

All routers maintain internally something called a *routing table*, this table is a quick reference guide for the router to know what to do with the request that it has been passed. For example, we know that our Roomba cat video lives at an IPv4 address of 172.16.121.15[1] (quite how we have obtained that information is something that we will cover in later chapters when we talk about DNS and name servers, but for now, we know that it is where we need to look for our video), so our request starts its journey to finding out where this IP address is physically located.

Step 1: Ask the computer that we are using:

Even the computer (or other device) that we are using contains a router of sorts and it too maintains a routing table of IP addresses that it is interested in. So essentially, in our case we are asking the computer "Is this you?" obviously the answer will come back as being no. And this is where the first use of our previously-mentioned interface comes into play. Our computer knows that the IP address is not itself, so it needs to route that request; it does this by routing it via its external interface.

Normally for a computer, that external interface will be connected via an Ethernet cable to our ISP-supplied router or modem, or it will be a Wi-Fi connection to the local access point.

Step 2: Ask our local router

With our request for our IP address having been passed from the computer or device that we are using to the local router, it will then handle the request in the same way as our computer did: as the request comes in, it will consult its routing table to

---

[1] This IP address has been used to illustrate the concept, it is actually a "private" IP address and does not really route to a location on the Internet but does serve to demonstrate the concept. With all Internet-accessible IP addresses having been assigned at the time of writing, using a random IP address could inadvertently route to a company or web resource which may be inappropriate or may not be allowed by the owner of that IP address.

see whether it finds a match to an internal resource (which would indicate that the video lives somewhere on your internal network), and that answer too will come back as “No”, hence your local router will pass the request to its external interface, which will be the telephone jack plugged into the wall, the other end of which will be a server at your ISP’s data centre.

Step 3: Let the ISP deal with it

Although in essence the way that your ISP’s server deals with the request is essentially the same as your local router deals with it, theirs is a more complete routing table to consult and considerably more external interfaces to route through.

Hitherto, the computer we are using and the local router have only really had two choices to deal with in terms of the incoming request: either I know how to deal with it or I don’t. If I don’t then I will pass it on to the next in line. Your ISP’s server (and all subsequent servers on the journey to the ultimate end destination) have to be a little more specific; rather than just getting to a response of “I don’t deal with it, pass it on to the next step”, it must be “I don’t deal with it, but this router can”. Hence, the routing tables of these servers will be along the lines of “For IP addresses that look like they fall between 0.0.0.0 and 100.255.255.255, send the requests through external interface ‘A’, for IP addresses that fall between 101.0.0.0 and 150.255.255.255 send the requests though external interface ‘B’, send IP addresses between 151.0.0.0 and 175.255.255.255 through external interface ‘C’” and so on.

We know from our destination IP address of 172.16.121.15 that we are going to have our request routed through external interface ‘C’

Step 4: Narrow down the requests until we find the correct router for our needs

The router on the other end of external interface ‘C’ will go through the same process as our ISP’s server, but it is dealing with more specific items in its routing table as it is only dealing with 151-175.x.x.x addresses; its routing table will route based upon the first and second octets of the IP address, so 151.0.x.x – 151.255.x.x will go through external interface ‘A’, 152.0.x.x – 152.255.x.x will go through external interface ‘B’ and so on.

Therefore, the next leap for our IP address is whatever external interface deals with all requests for 172.16.x.x. When we get to that router, it will have routing tables that deal with the first, second and third octets, and our request will go through whichever external interface is dealing with 172.16.121.x.

Now we get to the penultimate step in the chain because the router that was pointed to for the 172.16.121.x request will be routing for the entire IP address, and will respond with “Yes, you are looking for 172.16.121.15 and that is a request that I know about”, it will therefore route the request not through the external interface, but through an internal one because the requested resource (our Roomba cat video) exists on hardware that it can contact directly.

The final step therefore is to route requests to the specified IP address directly to the server that can deal with it; that server will then act like the local router in your office; it will know all of the IP addresses that it has locally and will deal with it as applicable.

So although we have used a bunch of words to get there, we can see that the journey that our IP address takes to get from us to the resource location is very similar to the way in which we would go to visit out client on the other side of the world – each step is becoming more and more specific until we reach the destination.

What you should bear in mind with the above is that it has been greatly simplified for illustrative purposes, and for reasons of efficiency in requests, the various servers along the way will learn the direct routes to the resources that we need as best they can so as to not have to do these convoluted routes all the time. So for example, if you were looking for a resource from a very popular website like Google or Facebook or something, then your ISP would know the IP address of the router that deals with it and therefore is able to skip all of the lookup in the middle which makes the requests that much quicker. Quite when and how that happens though is not something that you need to know about unless you want to go find out, but it is well beyond the scope of this book that's for sure.

With the above knowledge safely in the back pocket and a route to our resource of choice plotted and stored, can we now feast upon the unending delights of moggy atop robot vacuum? Well, no, not yet: all we know is where our feline friend and its trusty steed have stored the video evidence of them going into battle, now we have to get that video from where it currently resides to the device upon which we would like to watch it. And it's considerably more complicated than pressing the save buttons. Like everything else though, I'll keep it quite simple and see how we get along.

Welcome to the world of *packets* and *packet-switching*.

One of the perennial complaints from people using the Internet is that it is just too slow sometimes, and depending upon which country you are in, your definition of too slow may well be different to that of someone elsewhere in the world. However, we are all too familiar with the video clip that we are watching stuttering or even stopping midway though, the radio show that we are listening to just stops, or the Skype call goes crackly or just stops. That happens because the content being sent from one side of the transaction (the sender) does not reach the other side of the transaction (the recipient) in time, and whatever device you are using to view, listen, talk or whatever, does the best it can which is to stop doing anything.

The question then becomes why? We know where this resource lives, why isn't everything just available to us immediately.

Every resource that we need from the Internet contains a certain amount of data – a certain number of bits and bytes (words which we briefly introduced in an earlier chapter); the more of those bits and bytes there are in the resource, the more that has to be transferred to your device in order to deal with it correctly. Internet connections have a finite speed, the data can only travel along the wires at a certain maximum speed, and those wires can only cope with so much simultaneous data going back and forth along them. With something like our cat-laden vacuum cleaner video for example, that is a whole heap of data to transfer in order for us to have our few moments of laughter, and to have that transferred to our device takes time. We could sit and wait for all of those bytes to be transferred before we started watching, and for a short video that might take a minute or two to complete, but if you were looking to watch a feature length movie, that download process might take about the same time as the movie runs for, and wasting that time before you can even start to watch makes for a very poor user experience.

Those of you reading this, who, like me, are old enough to remember when the Internet was first around, may remember connecting over a modem and waiting for the smallest picture to be displayed on screen: it would gradually build itself, line by line on the screen until complete; it was an infuriating process to suffer. It does however illustrate quite well that the resources being served up are not done in a single block, they are split into smaller chunks called *packets*.

By sending the content we want in packets, we can not only start to utilise them quicker on our device – in the example of our video, we could start to watch the first couple of seconds whilst packets containing the next few seconds are sent to us in the background – but there is some fault tolerance that can be built into the system.

The Internet is a global network, it spans the entire globe, and if we would like to get our desired resource from the other side of the world (as we would often do even if it were unbeknown to us), then those bits and bytes must be transmitted along wires that also span the globe; it's a fair number of miles that our data covers. For sure, for the majority of the journey it is travelling along optic fibres at the speed of light, but we are also not the only people using those fibres and cables; we have to share that space with others doing whatever it is that they want to do. The result of that sharing is that given there are a finite amount of wires and fibres in existence there is congestion. Just like when we went to visit our client on the other side of the world a little earlier on, we could very easily hit peak hour traffic on the motorway and our progress would slow considerably or possibly even come to a complete standstill.

When we are travelling to our client and we hit a snag like this, we can usually reroute and use some alternate motorway or other road to get around the problem, it may not be the shortest route but in the end it is quicker. The routers on the Internet do the same sort of thing, as well as maintaining a list of which IP addresses exist through which interface, they also maintain metrics about how busy certain interfaces are, and how quickly data that is sent along that interface is received (routers know this information because each time a packet is passed between points, the receiving device sends back an acknowledgement of receipt to the sender which the sender logs and timestamps). Like with a road network, there are often many ways to get to a single point; there are tens of thousands of routers all around the world and seeing as they all do the same job of maintaining their routing tables to get a packet into or out of their network, they can all be used to route packets. If an external interface starts to get bogged down with too much activity and the response times fall below an acceptable level, the router will start to send packets that would normally go down interface 'A' to be dealt with, down interface 'B' instead and have the router at that end route them properly. This process is known as *packet switching.*

With these packets flying all around the world and potentially all taking different routes, our receiving device needs to recompile them back into a sensible order so that, in our example, the video is played in the correct sequence. This is done by essentially numbering the packets as the server sends them so that the recipient can organise them as they arrive.

Not all packets arrive. There are any number of reasons why, but some just get lost in the ether – swallowed up by a random router somewhere along the line. Mostly this will go completely unnoticed because the missing packet is detected by the sending router (having not received an acknowledgement of delivery), and sent again. This happens so quickly (usually) that it's as if the packet never went astray in the first place. But sometimes it doesn't happen quickly. Sometimes, for myriad reasons the packet just cannot be delivered despite the best efforts of our trusty router and we as users notice it at that point. That time when your YouTube video freezes for a second, or your Skype call drops a word, or maybe that one time out of a thousand when you look at your favourite webpage and the styling has gone completely. All signs of dropped packets. Of course all can also be caused by other problems, but they can be signs of dropped packets. Lost packets are nothing to worry about, they are a fact of Internet life, and there are mechanisms in place to deal with them, just know that there is not a 100% success rate with this stuff.

Packet switching is at the very heart of how the Internet works and without it the Internet just wouldn't work, it's that simple. Routers make packet switching possible, and those routers rely on IP addresses to know not only where a given resource is around the mass of data that is the Internet, but they know a way to get there too.

That's how in its most simplistic sense data gets sent around the Internet, how the information that lives on a server half way around the world ends up on your screen; there is a lot to it, many moving parts and it is an amazing feat of engineering that it has been made to work, and to work so well and so reliably as it does, every second of every single day. So, the next time the thing you need from the Internet isn't being delivered to you as you like, you'll still be quite annoyed by it, but you'll understand a little bit as to why it might be.

Chapter 5: Domain names

Domain names: The human-readable part of the Internet

So far everything we have mentioned about the Internet has been in the form of numbers: IP addresses. However, that's not the way we (as people) actually use the Internet in our day-to-day lives; that's mostly because we are just pretty bad at dealing with numbers. What we use are words, and for the Internet, those words mean *domain names.* Finally, a word that most of us would have heard of in the past. Cue the sighs of relief throughout the land.

The thing is, we use these domain names quite regularly but most people know nothing about them; they have no idea where they come from, how they are constructed, or when they can be used – most people are not even aware that they are case insensitive (that is, a domain name in all capital letters is the same as one in lower case), and the concept of the "www" part is a complete mystery – when is it used, when is it not? Most people also think that it is either just part of the domain name, or it is a requirement for the Internet to work. Both of which, as you will soon find out in more detail, are wrong.

But why am I going on about something that is seemingly so obvious? Well, if you were one of the people who were unaware of the case insensitivity or the situation around www, and you are also in the position of being an owner or manager of a small business, then it would be good for you to understand in more detail that thing upon which potentially a large chunk of your business depends.

Let us therefore dive more deeply – but again, not so deeply that we will never again see the light of day – into domain names. And fortunately it is nowhere near as complex, or involved, as packet switching was!

We don't live in a world of numbers, give me names

For those of you who don't know, a domain name is the name given to the address you end up at when you go to a website. For example, if you visit Google's website to conduct a search or to use one of the many tools that they make available, you'll be looking at a website named Google.com or Google.com.au or some other variant depending upon which part of the world you are in. Each of those variants is called the domain name. Other examples of domain names could be Yahoo.com, bt.com, myfavouritecatwebsite.de. I am sure that you will recognise the format because they are shown everywhere nowadays.

Domain names are used because people are just really bad at remembering numbers; it doesn't matter which language you speak, you do so using words (for the most part, sometimes sounds, but mostly words), we do not converse in numbers. In order for us to be able to get the resource(s) that we are interested in from the Internet, it is much easier and more convenient for us to type in a word that we can easily associate with what we are looking for, than to enter an IP address for the site that we want, especially if that IP address happens to be an IPv6 style - you'll remember the state of those numbers from when we looked at them a few chapters back. Domain names are a human readable representation of those IP addresses. The concept is entirely analogous to that of the contacts list in your mobile phone, or your buddy list in Skype: what's the betting that when you want to call your mum, you don't dial in the number of her phone (although it's the one number you should remember ... you have called her recently, haven't you?), you're going to scroll through the list of contacts and click her name.

It's just easier to remember the word "mum" and look it up in the helpfully alphabetical list than to recall the numbers. Even if you were able to recall your mum's phone number – and well done to you if you can – by the time a handful of various phone numbers have been committed to memory, the poor human brain is usually at its bursting point and about to give up completely, whereas some figures suggest that the average adult has a vocabulary of words in the 20-35,000 range. They are all basically random words but can be easily memorised; you try that with the same number of random numbers of equal length and see whether you can even get to 1% of that number, most people would fail miserably.

So long story short: domain names are human readable interpretations of the IP addresses that websites and other Internet-based resources use. There is of course a mechanism to translate from the domain name that we understand to the IP address that the Internet needs, but we'll get onto that in a future chapter.

Reading and understanding a domain name

You'd think that this would be about the end of the story when it comes to your domain name – it exists, and there you go. There is some kind of link between the domain name itself and the IP address to which it connects, but we'll get onto that, so what else could I possibly wish to know?

Simply, heaps.

We'll start by saying that most people completely misunderstand what a domain name is: they will usually get it mixed up with a web address (officially called a *Universal Resource Locator*, or *URL* for short) or, as alluded to previously, will start by quoting "www" at you, and all of these are wrong.

When we see an address of a resource on the Internet (and most commonly that address would be in the address bar of your browser), it will look something like the following:

https://www.mycatvideowebsite.de/files/showvideo?id=vacuumcat

It looks fairly straightforward doesn't it, not something that you haven't seen a million times before, but which part is the domain name, and what are all the other bits if they are not the domain name?

Those of you who mouthed (if not actually said out loud) that the domain name was mycatvideowebsite.de then give yourself a gold star, that is indeed the domain name.

What we are actually looking at above, in its entirety, is a URL, not a domain name. A domain name is only a part of the entire URL. Before we move on, let's take a very brief look at the remaining parts of the URL so that you know what they mean as this will enable the location of a domain name in any URL that you come across in the future. Now you may be asking why this is relevant. Well, remember that we are in the situation where our pizza-loving, coffee-swigging, neck-bearded IT guy is not currently available, your website is now doing something really strange, and remember that the buck stops with you to fix it. This is your company, so it is likely that you are going to be the one on the phone to the local 'IT fix-it' place and they are going to need to know some information, it's best to be prepared.

URLs are always read from left to right becoming more specific as to the location of the resource required the further to the right we go. Of course there are a number of languages, especially in the Middle East, that read and write from right to left. In those countries they would type the URL into the address bar of their browser in their native right to left format, but the browser will (internally) switch that around. Since 2010,

URLs can be written in non-Latin characters (such as Hebrew, Arabic or Chinese), but for the purposes of this book we will be sticking to English.

Reading left to right, the constituent parts of our URL are as follows:

https://

This is called the protocol; it is the HOW part of a request to an Internet-based resource. Quite what it does and how it does it is well beyond the scope of this book, but there is plenty of information available if you choose to go looking for it. You will generally see one of two protocols in a URL, being http:// and https://. Occasionally you may see ftp:// as the protocol which is specifically used in relation to moving files back and forth. There are loads of other protocols but you will probably never see them so there is no point in dwelling on them here.

There is an important point about protocols though, which as at the time of writing (2016), is very quickly becoming more and more relevant, and will only continue to do so, and that is the importance of the 's' at the end of the https:// protocol notation. That "s" signifies that the connection is secure and cannot be intercepted and read between sender and receiver. It is very quickly becoming the case that a secured protocol (namely https://) is the de facto communication protocol on the Internet. It has also been mentioned by Google that they will be assigning a better search ranking to those sites that use a secured protocol than those which don't, so that is something to bear in mind.

As an aside: when accessing an Internet-based resource over a secured https:// connection, your web browser will often show a padlock icon somewhere to further re-inforce the point that it is secured. This is certainly something that you would want to insist upon seeing when conducting any financial transaction (whether buying or selling), or giving out personal information to a website. No https:// protocol and padlock should equal no transaction and no data.

If your website doesn't have a https:// connection and you are expecting your customers to divulge their personal information or pay you money online, then you will notice that many will refuse (and so they should); it's an easy fix, just talk to your hosting company – more on which in a few chapters' time – about getting a secure certificate and things may well improve on that front for you.

www.

As mentioned earlier, this is not part of the domain name; it is what is called a *sub-domain*, it signifies a small part of the larger domain. Domain names can be used (and very often are used) to cover all Internet-based activities of a company. Your website, although often the most visible part to the public, is just a small part of that activity. You may have services that you offer to clients over the Internet and that would usually still be done via your domain name, but is not your website. www sub-domains always indicate a website, but they are not necessary for one - this is something that we will cover in more detail in the next chapter when we discuss DNS.

It is entirely possible to have multiple levels of sub-domain in a URL, the more levels there are, the more refined the area of the domain is. Let's look at an example to illustrate that point, it's a little off topic but will help.

Imagine that we are not running a small business, but a large multi-national. Our fictitious company has offices all over the world and we are employing tens of thousands of staff, they all have laptops and desktop PCs, there are servers that enable our clients to use our services and so forth; we need to be able to identify those resources (laptops, desktop PCs and servers) very easily. It doesn't matter which office or part of the world those resources are in, they are all still part of our massive multi-national company. For the purposes of the exercise, we'll call our company "Massive Mega Co", and we have a domain name of "massivemega.co" (which at the time of writing didn't exist so there should be no erroneous linking to large multi-national companies by accident).

All of our online presence falls somewhere under the massivemega.co domain name. Our website is, naturally, www.massivemega.co, but we need to be able to identify resources, not a website, so we'll create a sub-domain for the purpose. Let's call it "resources".

So, our big group of worldwide resources is identified as resources.massivemega.co

That rather puts all of our resources into one big bucket and doesn't allow us to identify them easily, we need to break it down a bit more. This could be done by creating what might be called a "sub-sub-domain", some people call these "2nd level sub-domains" but in reality, they are still just plain old sub-domains. Let's start by creating one for various areas of the world in which our PCs may exist, as follows:

asia.resources.massivemega.co

europe.resources.massivemega.co

usa.resources.massivemega.co

There we have two levels of sub-domain (asia.resources, europe.resources and usa.resources), they all reside "beneath" our main domain name. We could go still further if we wanted to – and this is not an unusual practise in large companies, in fact is it the norm for massive networks – we could have:

adelaide.asia.resources.massivemega.co

There is no limit (realistically) to the number of sub-domains that a domain can actually have, for example:

firstfloor.adelaide.asia.resources.massivemega.co is still valid, and so it goes on.

The takeaway here is that regardless of the number of sub-domains shown in a URL, the domain name itself is still the same, it is still: massivemega.co

Which does rather beg the question as to how you would identify the main domain name and the sub-domains in a URL. That's a little bit more difficult to answer because it's something that you learn with experience, and the trick is to learn what is in the URL after the domain name. Once you know what can come after a domain name in a URL (and there are only a few possibilities, with one of those possibilities being nothing), the domain name itself is always the item just before it.

mycatvideowebsite.de

This is our main domain name, the part of the URL that this entire chapter is dedicated to. What we notice about our domain name to start with is that it has a full stop (or period) in it. In fact, it can have a few but we'll get to that in just a second.

Essentially the domain name is made up of two parts; our main name on the left hand side (mycatvideowebsite in the example) and what is called a *Top Level Domain* or *TLD* on the right hand side. All domain names must include a top level domain; as the name implies, a Top Level Domain is the "root" of all domain names that we see on the Internet today, and is a way in which responsibility for assigning domain names to customers could be shared around the world and not left in the hands of a single body (there is an overarching single body that controls the Top Level Domains but that is information for another time).

The most popular Top Level Domain by far is ".com", but there are hundreds of others that can be used, from the fairly well known ".net" to the more recent and more specialised ".travel" and many more besides. As well as these generic words that act as Top Level Domains, there are also ones which are country-specific, and they would usually end in the ISO code[2] of the country concerned. Our example domain name for this section of the book is mycatvideowebsite.de, with the Top Level Domain being ".de", which happens to be for Germany. If the domain name were registered in Poland, it may be ".pl", or in Australia, ".au".

To make life just a little bit more confusing, a Top Level Domain doesn't have to be a single word, it can be multiple words but only in the case of country-specific Top Level Domains; there are a few countries that have adopted this behaviour and below is a list of some which have. It is not a complete list by any means, but a list of those ones that you are more likely to see around and about:

.com.au and .net.au (as well as a few others) are in use in Australia

.co.nz is in use in New Zealand

.co.uk (and others) are in use in United Kingdom

.com.br is in use in Brazil

There are heaps more but it does demonstrate that the domain name is not quite as simple as it would at first appear and can actually be quite confusing. Rule of thumb would be that if the Top Level Domain ends in a two letter ISO country code then it could also have secondary part to it.

[2] ISO Stands for the International Organization for Standardization. As the name implies, they create standards for all sorts of things; in this instance, I am referring to their standard list of county abbreviations..

Having our Top Level Domain means that the same name can be registered in different countries and against different Top Level Domains because google.com is not the same as google.pl for example (although they probably go to the same website in the end, they are separate domain names).

We are going to talk about registration of domain names in a little while.

/files/video

Here we have what is called the "path" to the resource, it is like a signpost from the entry point of the website to where the resource we are looking for lives. Think of it like the board in a department store entrance that advises the shopper on which floor and in which direction the department of interest is: "toys and games, 3rd floor in a westerly direction from here".

Resources paths can take a few forms; they can be directory style resources like our one here (look in the "files" directory, then from there, the "video" directory), or they could specify a "page". If the path contains a full stop (or period) then it will be specifying a page. An example of that might be: www.mycatvideowebsite.de/files/playvideo.aspx - because we have a full stop in the path, (before the aspx at the end which is a file type, same as it is on your desktop or laptop), we are looking at a page style path.

Domain names may not contain most non alphanumeric characters such as slashes and question marks etc., so that makes it easier to identify where a domain name ends and a path starts.

?id=vacuumcat

Just a passing mention to this part of the URL because it is a) optional, b) entirely dynamic in nature, c) almost limitless in size and d) programmer speak.

These are called "*Query String Parameters*" and if they are present in a URL, they go right at the end and always start with a question mark. They are essentially name/value pairs of data that is being passed to the resource in question. In our example here, we are passing the ID of the video that we would like to play, that ID being "vacuumcat". It is possible to have multiple data passed in using this method and the various keys are separated by an ampersand symbol (&), so it would be entirely possible to have Query String Parameters as: ?id=vacuumcat&startAt=beginning.

Besides possibly having to recite these items at the end of a URL, you will have absolutely no use for them whatsoever and needn't worry about them. To your web developer or programmer though they are heaps of fun.

So that's how a URL is made up, and we can see that the domain name is actually only a very small part of it; to help you along your way in being able to identify a domain name within a URL as shown in the address bar of your web browser, you'll see nowadays that most, if not all, browsers will highlight in bold (or using some other method) the domain name within the address bar for you. This is an important security precaution actually because people have been known to fall for the occasional online scam which would often involve them visiting, and ultimately entering information into, a website that is not that which it is purporting to be. The most common examples of this are scammers sending their victim to a website designed to look like that of a financial institution in the hope of obtaining their login details and cleaning out their account. By highlighting the domain name in the address bar, it makes it easier to see that you are in fact on a website under the name of "dodgyscamartist.com" rather than "trustedbank.com". Something to keep an eye on for sure.

Obtaining and registering a domain name
As mentioned before, each domain name has a Top-Level Domain and each of these Top Level Domains is administered and maintained by a company known as a registrar. It is from that registrar that one would obtain the domain name for our company.

For the most part registrars do not deal directly with registrants – that is to say, you. All of your dealings will be through a reseller organisation which more often than not would be your web hosting company or a domain name retailer on the Internet. You would request your desired domain name with them, they would check the list of existing domain names and if your desired name has not already been registered then they will register it with the registrar on your behalf.

Domain names (for those working with a Standard English character set) must contain only letters, numbers or a hyphen. They are not case sensitive, so mycatvideowebsite.de is the same as MYCATVIDEOWEBSITE.DE, and although there is a minimum length (2 characters, all combinations of which are already taken within almost every TLD), there is no realistic maximum length. The absolute maximum length for a URL including absolutely everything in your web browser's address bar is 1024 characters, but a domain name would be nowhere near long enough to approach that sort of a limit. If you are considering, or have, a domain name that has even 50 characters in it, then you should seriously consider your options as people will get that wrong almost every time.

What is very important to note at this time is that you never actually OWN the domain name that you register; it is always owned by the registrar. What you do own is the exclusive rights to use it. You get to lease it for a period of time; not less than one year, and normally not more than 10 years at a time. At the end of that rental period you can either choose to renew the domain name rental for another period, or let the name lapse. If lapsed, a previously registered domain name could be registered by a different qualifying entity, so therefore, if you have a domain name that you are quite keen on keeping, don't let it expire.

There are safeguards in place to prevent a domain name from expiring but this is one of those times where you, as the owner or manager of a small business, absolutely MUST know when your domain name(s) is/are expiring and you also MUST know the reseller that was used to purchase them initially.

Be warned, if a domain name expires for long enough, it is just turned off, then your world stops. Completely. And as I mentioned in the introduction to this book, that is not the time to be learning about this sort of stuff, and not the time to be scrambling around trying to find that sort of information out because your IT guy who set it all up for you initially has moved on to pastures, and pizzas, new.

Restrictions on ownership

As I mentioned previously, your domain name can be whatever you want it to be – provided it is currently available for registration - but that doesn't mean that absolutely anybody can register anything. In some, but not all instances, there are rules.

One of the most common rules for a TLD that is specific to a country for example, is that in order to register a domain using that TLD, you must live or work or do business in that country.

Australia is such an example: to register a .com.au domain (the main TLD for Australia), you must meet that criteria, and also you must have a business number or ABN which means that an individual cannot easily register a domain name. Odd, but true. Besides country-specific TLDs that have restrictions, there are some generic TLDs that have restrictions upon who can register them: .travel is another good example, not just anyone can register one of those, you must be a fully functioning and recognised travel-related company, and they do undertake quite rigorous investigations to ensure that you are not making false claims. It is always wise to check the rules of a specific TLD with your reseller before you try to register a domain name and especially before you get to the stage of printing marketing materials in order to avoid disappointment.

Renewals

You now know that your chosen domain name isn't yours, you only rent it for a period of time – the minimum and maximum of which are set by the registrar that maintains the TLD in question, so eventually, that lease is going to expire.

As alluded to previously, when the expiration date comes around you can either choose to renew the domain or let it lapse.

As the renewal time comes around, your reseller – and possibly the registrar too – will start to send e-mails out to remind you that the domain name is due to expire. These e-mails will be sent to one of the contacts that was placed on the domain name at the time of initial registration so it is important that those contact details be kept current. Neither the registrar or reseller are responsible for tracking you down to let you know that your domain is going to expire if your contact e-mail address is wrong. If it is wrong then the first you will know about it, is when your domain name expires and your commercial world stops – along with your website and your e-mails.

When a domain name is first registered, the registrant will be asked to provide a number of contact points: a technical contact, administrative contact and billing contact. ALWAYS make sure that the administrative contact is an e-mail address that can be accessed by a number of people in your company, maybe an info@ or similar address. NEVER make this address that of your IT guy, because if your IT guy is gone, so are your renewal reminders and before long, so is your domain.

As we are talking about renewals, now is a good time to mention that just because you initially registered a domain with a certain company, doesn't mean that you are tied to that company for life. You can move domain names around between resellers very simply and within a few days and little to no impact on your website or e-mail; and usually without charge. The most cost effective time to switch between resellers, if that is your intention, is about two weeks prior to your domain name coming up for renewal.

The name I want is taken. What can I do?

Although it is possible to choose any domain name you want, everyone else has the same possibility to do so. You may have been in business for 100 years, but that doesn't give you any special privileges when it comes to domain registration. It's a first come, first served situation, so you'll need to be on the ball.

However, if your business, or just the domain name you want, is a generic or popular word or name, then the chances are that the domain you want – especially in the more common TLDs like .com – is taken, so what can you do.

There are a few options available to you, but this book is not the time to be discussing them in any great detail; you're better off going to your reseller and asking their advice. It is possible that the domain name has been leased by someone with the intention of selling that lease to someone, such as you, in specific need of it, for the purposes of making money. If so, you may be able to do a deal with the current leaseholder. For the most part though, if the name is taken then it is taken. You could wait until it is up for renewal and see whether the current lease is renewed, if it isn't then you can grab it on a first come, first served basis again. Usually though, if your domain name is taken, the only available option is to think of a new one I am afraid.

Multiple domains for a single website

It is certainly not uncommon for a company to have multiple domain names pointing to a single website, it happens all the time, and unless there are rules laid down by the domain registrar specifically preventing ownership of multiple domains, then go for your life, get all the ones you can. In fact, there are often very good reasons for grabbing multiple domain names for your business. For instance, you may be contemplating some huge marketing push which uses a certain word or phrase, registering that word or phrase can help in promotion of that event. There was a very large car manufacturer who did just this sort of thing to great effect, they registered not only their marque's domain but the tagline from their commercials. The voiceover for the commercials used the tagline all the time and there it was as the still image at the end: the tagline.com or whatever the TLD was. Very clever. However, this is not a book about marketing so we'll push on.

In the upcoming chapter when we discuss DNS and specifically Name Servers, you'll learn how it is easily possible to have any number of domain names point at your website.

Chapter 6: The phonebook

DNS: Turning words into numbers
With the IP addresses on the one hand which the computers of the Internet understand, and the domain names on the other hand that we understand, we need something that will translate from one to the other. Specifically, we need a lookup of IP addresses based upon domain names; we need a phone book.

The Internet has its own phonebook, it's a system known as *DNS* which stands for *Domain Name System* (sometimes *Service* but usually System). It is the role of DNS – at its most basic level – to complete the simple lookup of domain name to IP address so that you can easily watch the cat video on your favourite player site, but the Internet contains much more than just websites. Of course websites are the most visible part of the system, they are the part that most of us would interact with every day, but another function of the Internet that is not only ubiquitous but basically vital in todays connected world, is e-mail. E-mail travels over the same Internet that your website of choice does, so how does the DNS system know that it is your intention to write to your Great Aunt Mildred, thanking her not only for the book token but the very generous gift of that oversized jumper with the three arms, instead of hoovering up cat videos by the dozen from YouTube? Besides this, we have already learned that websites can be hosted on servers anywhere in the world, and we know how to find that server once we have the IP address, but what if the website is moved to a new server, how can that website be tracked once moved. The answer to both of these questions – and many more, as it turns out – is DNS, another pillar of the Internet that most people are completely oblivious to, but an understanding of it can get you out of trouble when the wheels fall off.

One item to note in relation to DNS is this: every domain name that you purchase the rights to use, must have a *DNS record* in order for that domain name to be accessible on the Internet (either for the purposes of hosting your website, or setting up e-mail with an address ending in "at" your domain name). Without it, there is no routing table for your web browser to query, and requests for the website at that domain name will result in a "site unavailable" message in your web browser, or your belated Christmas e-mail to Great Aunt Mildred will come bouncing back to you with an undeliverable message, usually advising you that the domain is unknown. This is what's called a hard bounce, and is something that we are going to look at in more detail in a later chapter, when we talk all about e-mail.

You don't need to specifically set this initial record up as one will be automatically created for you by the reseller from whom you initially rent the domain name, but you can modify it to suit your needs and can even move it around, but a DNS record will always be there. There are tools available on the Internet to lookup the content of this DNS record, the results of which we will look at in a little while, but one of the most common problems encountered by a company when their Internet goes down is that their domain name has expired, and this can be easily ascertained by checking to see whether the DNS record is available. If it isn't, there is a fair chance that your domain name has expired and there is no routing table to the IP address relating to your website server or e-mail server.

Types of DNS entries

We now know that we have this DNS record, and understand that it is the routing table for our domain name, but we don't quite know how it does the actual routing of a request. How does your web browser know that a www-prefixed domain name is a request for a website, and doesn't send you off into a pointless circle of trying to send an e-mail to it, or how does it know that test.mywebsite.com lives in a completely different location to www.mywebsite.com? And how does it know that www.mywebsite.com and www.mynewcompanyname.com should actually be looking at the same website? Now we have to dig a little deeper into how the DNS system actually works. It's actually very simple, it's just that some of the words and phrases may be new to you.

It's about now that the analogy with the phone book starts to break down just a little bit; where the phone book will generally only have one listing for our friendly, local car service centre, a DNS entry will have at minimum a handful of listings for them, but could potentially have hundreds of listings for them, all combined into the single record.

What does that mean though, how is that possible?

The DNS record itself is more of a table of what are called *entries*, there will be one entry in the DNS record for each type of request that may be received to the domain. So, there will be an entry there that matches incoming e-mail requests, and another for our www-prefixed website request, another for our domain name without the www prefix and so on. By looking up the correct entry in the DNS record, the Internet – and ultimately your web browser, or your e-mail client on your desktop or mobile application – knows where to look in order to obtain whatever resource it is that has been requested.

Let's then have a look at a very standard, but entirely fictitious[3] DNS record, and break it down a little bit so that everything that I have said thus far starts to make a little bit of sense.

---

[3] At the time of writing, neither mygreatdomain.co nor mywebhost.co were registered to any entity. They may have been registered between that time and the time you are reading this book, but any reference to any now registered domain is purely coincidental.

Text	Domain	Type	TTL	Answer
	mygreatdomain.co.	A	10800	172.16.121.15
	mygreatdomain.co.	NS	10800	ns1.mywebhost.co.
	mygreatdomain.co.	NS	10800	ns2. mywebhost.co.
	mygreatdomain.co.	SOA	10800	Minimum/NegTTL: 86400 Expire: 1209600 Retry: 600 Refresh: 3600 Serial: 2015041001 Responsible Name: hostmaster. mygreatdomain.co. Primary DNS server: ns1. mywebhost.co.
	mygreatdomain.co.	MX	10800	mail. mygreatdomain.co. [Preference = 10]
	mygreatdomain.co.	TXT	10800	"v=spf1 a mx -all"
www	mygreatdomain.co	A	10800	172.16.21.18
mail	mygreatdomain.co.	A	10800	172.16.121.15

When we first look at something like this it is a complete mess and jumble of random things, but you'll already know that nothing here is random, just not yet fully understood. Take a look at it again and you'll start to see some familiar things there staring out at you: we can see that towards the left, everything is referring to the domain name: mygreatdomain.com; we can also see some familiar looking IP addresses leaping out at us. For the most part at the moment, the rest is complete junk, but shortly, it will all come into a very clear focus.

For the remainder of this chapter, we are going to be referring to the content in this DNS record, so you might want to fold the corner of this page over or add a bookmark to it or something so that you can flip back and forth.

A quick note before we continue on though: if you were to look at a real DNS record using an online tool, it may look slightly different to the one you are currently looking at, for sure the data will be different, but the headings may be shown with different names and it may be laid out in a different fashion. None of that really matters though, because it's about how to read the record, and how the Internet reads the record. You should also note that the IP addresses shown are – for the purposes of illustration - all within private address ranges (as was mentioned when we went through IP addresses, so will not actually resolve to anything).

We're not going to examine the DNS record from left to right or anything like that, instead we are going to pick out items based upon their importance. The first thing to look at is the TYPE of entry, in our example under the heading of "Type". You'll see a few different codes: A, NS, SOA etc., these are the key to how DNS works really. Every type of request that comes into the DNS record will be for a specific type of entry, the DNS system will then return the "Answer" as shown here in our answer column. Sometimes, that will be an IP address as in the case here of our "A" entries, sometimes it will be a block of information as in the case here of the "SOA" and "TXT" entries, or it might be a pointer to another DNS record or entry in the current record, as per that of the "MX" entries.

There are dozens of these types that can appear in a DNS entry, each with a specific task. There is not much point in listing them all here because if it is something that you would like to know more about then there are copious articles online that can help you out. There are however a handful of types that are far more common and will be seen in almost every DNS record, as follows:

A and AAAA

These are both types of address record, for IPv4 addresses the A type is used whereas IPv6 addresses utilise the AAAA type. These would result in an IP address that your browser or application would then navigate to in order to obtain the resource required.

CNAME

This stands for a *Canonical Name Record* which is a fancy way of saying an alias, it would return the name of the aliased domain name which would force your browser to do another lookup to that aliased domain.

MX

Stands for *Mail Exchanger*, or, as we know it in the real world: e-mail. These records are checked when someone is looking to send you an e-mail, it will return a domain name which is the domain name of your mail sever.

NS

Name Server: the most important type in the list as it denotes what is known as the administrative server, which is something that we will be looking at later in this chapter.

PTR

A pointer; very similar in nature to a CNAME type but instead of doing another lookup like a CNAME would, a PTR type entry would just return the information in the answer column and no further action is taken.

SOA

Start of authority: all DNS records must have one of these entries, it has a brief summary of the most important information about the domain: primary name server, e-mail address of the administrative contact (see the chapter on Domain Names for the importance of this) and other such information.

TXT

Basically a general store of information about some or all of the domain, quite often used (in part) in relation to who may or may not send e-mails from this domain name (something called an SPF record, but that goes beyond the scope of this book), suffice to say that TXT type information is just returned to the calling party with no further action taken by that party.

Of course there are heaps of other entry types available, but these are the most common.

With all of these types, how do we know which one to pick? The request flow is like this (and bear in mind, this is a simplified example)

First of all, the "root" entry for a domain is requested. This is an entry of type "A" which just has a domain name, and nothing else to identify it. In our example, it is the top entry in the list (which is the place you will usually find it shown). That returns an answer which effectively means, if you cannot find what you are looking for specifically, go to this IP address and see whether that server can help you out.

Once the root entry has been obtained, the specific entry of interest is requested – that will be done by a combination of the entry type (A, MX, TXT whatever) and any sub-domain (www etc.). The result of that lookup must be either no matching entry (in which case the request is routed off to the IP address obtained from the root entry) or a single entry matching our search. As you can see from the details in the various entry types above, we can get one of three answers to our request:

1. We can be given some information (as in the case of TXT or SOA etc. entries). In this case that is returned to the calling party and the transaction is finished.
2. We can be given an IP address to look at to find the resource that we are looking for, where our browser will go and try to access the resource in question from that IP address. This would be the case in an A or an AAAA type entry amongst others, or finally,
3. We get a redirection notification. If a redirection is returned (as would be the case with a CNAME, PRT or MX type entry) then another request is made to the DNS record requesting the resource that we have been redirected to. Around and around the process goes until either information or, more likely, an IP address is returned, where the request is then routed.

Ignoring the return of information scenario, because it is just not something that you need to know about here, let's look at the two most common types of requests that a DNS record receives, using our sample DNS record above.

Luckily, the two most common types of request (website and e-mail) demonstrate both of these concepts perfectly, so we'll go through them one at a time. Starting with the request for a website.

- The web browser is looking to go to mygreatdomain.co (or, www.mygreatdomain.co as we'll look at how both work)
- For a start off, we get the root entry (remember, that's the one with a type of A, but no other information), so

that if we cannot find the entry we are looking for, then that's the IP address that we will route to

In the case of requesting our website without the www sub-domain, that's where it ends, we've got the information that we need and the request will be routed. When we have our domain name with the www sub-domain, then we need to make an additional request:

- We look for an entry with a type of "A" and a sub-domain (shown in our example in the "text" column) of www. This returns us an IP address and the request is routed appropriately.

What you will notice here is that the root entry and the www record both return the same IP address, which is how a website can be retrieved (usually) with or without the www prefix. If you are finding that your website will only work in either one of those situations, but not both, then your DNS record is missing one of those entries.

It should be noted that the explanation given of the redirection here is slightly abridged for the sake of clarity, as the requests are a little more involved because sub-domains actually have their own DNS records. This makes the system infinitely flexible, but incredibly difficult to show to people new to the concept for the first time, that is why a web hosting company will often add the sub-domain entries into a DNS record for you through their control panel.

Now that we have done the website look up, we can move on to the sending of mail. It is, in essence, exactly the same procedure except this time, after the initial root record look up we are not looking for an "A" entry but for the Mail Exchanger or "MX" entry.

A DNS record may actually have multiple MX entries – if you are a user of Google for your mail services for example, your DNS record will probably contain about five MX entries. Besides always being redirection type answers, you'll notice that MX entries also have numbers with them – in our example it is labelled as preference, but could equally be labelled as weight – and are usually shown within square brackets. This weighting or preference is a clue to the Internet as to which of the MX entries to use first (the one with the lowest weight is used first – they are often weighted in tens although that is not a requirement, so 10 would be used before 20 which is before 30 and so on). The reason that multiple MX entries can be stored is to handle the destination mail server being unavailable at the time of request. Therefore, if the mail server specified for the MX entry with a weight of 10 is unavailable, another lookup is made for the next lowest weighted MX and that is then tried. This process is repeated until either an available mail server is found and the message delivered, or no more MX entries are found when the request denied and the e-mail is bounced after attempting to deliver it to the IP address at the root record (which will usually always fail).

To get to our mail example then, we go through the following steps:

- Lookup the root entry, to get our fall back route
- Lookup the MX entry with the lowest weight (in our example, we only have one, so get that) which returns a redirection result. For us, it points to mail.mygreatdomain.co
- Lookup the A type entry for mail.mygreatdomain.co which would normally result in an IP address, so route to that

If the IP address is unavailable, go back and get the next MX entry and repeat until we either succeed or fail.

How and why DNS is spread around the world

There we go then, we now have a reasonable understanding of how the DNS works, and we can now see how we are able to translate our request for a website from the domain name that we understand, into an IP address that the Internet understands. We can also see how the Internet is able to differentiate between a request for a website, and a request for an e-mail account, and with this knowledge can extrapolate it out quite easily to understanding how all requests on the Internet for absolutely anything can be made.

Where we find ourselves now though is staring down the barrel of another question. Sorry about that. The question is: I have this DNS record and it's set up perfectly to route all of the requests that I could possibly receive, but how does the Internet know where to look to find it, and how do I advise the Internet that I have this fantastic DNS record just sitting there, waiting to be used, and pointing to an even more amazing website that is going to make me a fortune?

Enter from stage left: Name Servers.

DNS records live on name servers; these are specially configured servers which would usually be controlled by either a specialist DNS hosting company, your web hosting company or maybe even your ISP. Their role in the Internet is effectively to publish a list of domain names for which it is responsible. In essence, publicising a statement saying "I know everything there is to know about mygreatdomain.co and its DNS entries, if you want to know about that, come talk to me".

Fantastic, that's exactly what we need – an Internet signpost to get us started. Except, no. Sadly. Having a name server that is responsible for pointing the Internet in the right direction is great, but if you have a very popular name server that finds itself responsible for THE site of the moment then it is very quickly going to get swamped. Imagine how many requests there are every second, let alone every minute, hour or even day, for sites like Google, Microsoft, Apple, Facebook and Twitter. Even if a name server were only responsible for one of those sites it would quickly become overloaded with requests. Yes, more servers can be added, but the requests keep coming and we end up with what's called a single point of failure because there is only one source of information. If that disappears then all of the information about the domain goes with it. What happens if that name server – for whatever reason – no longer advertises the fact that it is responsible for Facebook's DNS record? The Facebook site is still up and running but nobody can use it because the DNS entries are not available because the name server has blown a fuse or whatever. Not the ideal situation.

Instead what we have on the Internet is a distributed set of name servers; we have the one upon which our main DNS record resides, but there are tens of thousands (in some cases) of copies of these records on servers all around the world, thereby removing the single point of failure in our own name server.

To explain it in a little more detail, we need to go through the steps that a packet of data actually goes through in order to get you from staring at a blank screen, to being able to advise your adoring Facebook friends, all 20,000 of them, that you now know how DNS works ... kind of.

We're going to start with the packet leaving your computer and heading towards the router in your network – this will be the box that your ISP gave you, or your IT guy bought and installed for you – which connects you to the Internet. Inside of that router, there is basically a table of local IP addresses on your network. When the data packet comes into the router from your computer, it checks the tables to see whether it can be delivered locally. It's a request to find out where the Facebook site lives, so the answer is no. Next step, is that it redirects the packet to your ISP ... they are on the other end of the wire that plugs into the wall, and they have a router too (except theirs is bigger and faster than yours); the packet comes in asking where Facebook lives. Now, if yours is the first request for Facebook then the answer is "No, I don't have that here, but I do know the name server that can tell me"; at which point your request will be forwarded on to the name server, the IP address will be obtained and away you go, off and running. However, if yours is not the first request for Facebook, then the answer comes back as, "Yes, I know exactly where to point you for that", the IP address is returned and you are off and running again. Of course, in reality the actual process is more involved, but this helps to understand the principal. The bottom line is that although there is only one authoritative name server for a domain which holds the main DNS record, there are potentially thousands of copies of the information on countless servers around the world in an effort to reduce the number of data packets flying around looking for information that really doesn't change very often. In general practise, once DNS is set up it rarely changes. This process is called "caching", and DNS records are "cached" at various locations throughout the process ... they are cached by your web browser, then sometimes by your local router, certainly by your ISP and so on.

The problems of different DNS record versions

We now know that there are these myriad copies around the world of our precious DNS record because it rarely changes, but rare changes are not no changes at all, so what happens to those copies around the world? If they are only updated when the first request comes, then they could be years out of date.

True, if they were only updated on that basis, but they are not.

It is up to the owner of the DNS server that is caching the data to update the records thereon at an interval that suits their needs, but again, that could lead us to the same problem: if that owner only updated their information infrequently, or, for whatever reason, our DNS records are updated on a frequent basis, we are back to square one quite quickly with out of date records. This is where the next column in our example record comes into play, it's called TTL.

TTL, which stands for Time-To-Live, is the key to how long the DNS record is cached for. Essentially, it is a pledge on your part (as the DNS record owner) to say, "The most frequently that I will ever update my DNS record is this number of seconds, so feel free to keep it for anything up to this period, then throw it away", and this gets us out of trouble. At any time from the point at which the DNS record was retrieved until the number of seconds has elapsed, the cached copy of the DNS record will be considered valid. At the point the number of seconds elapses, the cached version is thrown away and the next time a request is made, the process starts over.

Of course, this leads us to the possibility of a DNS record having a huge TTL and therefore becoming stale, or someone setting a very low TTL so that the data is always being re-fetched from the name server. Both of these situations have of course been thought of in the past, and there are safe-guards in place: for the former situation, the TTL is a maximum and the caching DNS server can choose to discard the information earlier if it wants to, which covers the stale data scenario, and to have the TTL really low so that it is continually updating from live is covered by a minimum TTL imposed by the same caching servers. There are a few domains that can request and obtain lower TTLs because their data changes so frequently, but if you are reading this book, you can be absolutely sure that your domain ain't one of them.

The takeaway from this is that if you need to make DNS changes – because your site is being hosted in a new location, or you have added a sub-domain or changed your mail exchanger or something - then be aware that not everywhere around the world will get the changes you make immediately; your domain could have a standard TTL of 10800 seconds (or 3 hours) and the latest enquiry could have gotten their cached copy 1 second before your record was changed, hence, it's going to be three hours as a minimum before they come asking you again for your latest entry. Allow time for the DNS changes to be updated in all of the cached copies, maybe make the change last thing at night so that they are ready to go the following morning or something. Perhaps, if the change is more critical and you have some warning, you could lower the TTL a few days in advance, so that cached copies expire quicker, then your propagation time will be shorter. Remember to reset the TTL back to normal when you are finished though because the additional packet traffic can be done without.

Failover and backup DNS entries

What if there is a problem with my name server – my DNS entries will not be returned, and my domain could appear offline to any number of visitors and potential clients?

If we look back at our original DNS record, we can see that – in this case – it specifies two name servers (identified as a type of NS); and this accounts for that very situation. Usually, the name server listed first will be consulted, but if it is not available then the second one will be brought into play, in exactly the same way as DNS does for the Mail Exchanger (MX) records. In the case of name servers, each DNS record MUST have at least two, and that is the standard number that are added to a record, but they can have up to six in some instances but this is rare. Mostly you'll see between two and four.

Chapter 7: Hosting services

Hosting services: Investing the big bucks for you

We've spent a bit of time now looking at the nuts and bolts of the Internet, trying to make some sense of all the puzzle pieces and work out where they fit in the overall picture. With that grounding knowledge in place we are now able to move on to the fun stuff – the bits of the Internet that actually have some kind of tangible result. Basically, the bits that you and others can see and interact with; realistically, the bits that bring the Internet to life and make it usable.

Hosting services and what they provide

What we've seen so far is a bunch of relatively disparate services: from the well-known Domain Name on the one hand to the not so well known IP addresses on the other, via the DNS in the middle that acts as the glue to it all; and we've talked – rather nonchalantly as it turns out – about servers for DNS and servers to act as name servers and caching servers, this, that and the other. What we haven't talked about is where are all these servers, do they actually exist in the physical world, is it something that – should you felt the inclination to – you could walk up and touch? If so, who has to purchase them and where are they located? With all of these servers banded around quite merrily as we have been seeing in the previous chapters, as a small business owner, there is a worryingly large invoice busily honing into view at the thought of all this kit, and that's before we think about who is responsible for maintaining them all, and keeping out the dreaded security flaws and so on.

This is the point of the play where your web hosting company enters the frame. It is their job to abstract you from the minutia of how the stuff that we have looked at actually works in practise. They've already made the investment in the physical server kit – known as hardware – and more importantly, the infrastructure to tie them all together. They have all of the responsibility of ensuring that your name servers are there to respond when the request comes from your potential customer, and that DNS records are available for the world to see and cache. They act as the broker between you and the registrar when obtaining your domain names, and more important than all that, they have already made the investment in the all-important IP address that your website so desperately needs in order to be visible on the Internet.

In short, a web hosting company has done all of the hard work so all you have to do is remember to pay them and the lights to your Internet world remain burning brightly.

Single host for everything or multiple hosts

As with pretty much everything in life, when it comes to dealing with a hosting company there are thousands to choose from; all offering pretty much the same sort of thing, all at pretty much the same sort of cost (for the most part), so how do you choose? There is also the vexed question of whether we have a single hosting company that deals with everything for us, or do we try to find a couple of companies to share the load between them. We already know that there are a number of functions that we need to be on top of: registering our domain name; ensuring that DNS records are publicly visible and cacheable; making sure that there is a server available with sufficient capacity to host the website that is going to make you millions for being the next big thing; and ensuring that e-mail – the key to many businesses nowadays - continues to flow, so is that too much work and responsibility for a single hosting company? Have we run into another single point of failure? Or is splitting the functions out between multiple companies going to be more of an administration headache for us when we are already replete with headaches from running the company in the first place?

The reality is that it doesn't actually matter that much. A general hosting company will always tell you that it's best to have everything in one place for ease of management, whereas a specialist hosting company (one specialising in DNS hosting for example – as we will get on to shortly) will insist that because they only do one thing that they do it better than everyone else. There is no global right or wrong answer, it comes down to the needs of your business and how it moves and adapts to the markets in part too.

For the most part, the majority of the time people and especially small businesses, will choose to have all of their eggs in the one basket with a single hosting company to do everything for them. That way, there is a single point of contact in the event that the wheels fall off, there is not a whole bunch of chasing around trying to establish which company is responsible for which part of the puzzle, and there are fewer invoices each billing period and it's just easier.

The single hosting company approach will work in at least 90% of all cases. It's the remaining 10% where things start to get a little trickier; it is here where there are specific business needs (or potentially a company policy) to keep these items separate. Usually though, if you have multiple hosting companies, you will have someone in the company who is responsible for knowing which does what role.

The most common parts of the Internet puzzle that get off-loaded to specialist companies at the moment are e-mail and DNS. E-mail is usually hived off to a special company when storage becomes an issue, and in that case the most common route to take is moving to one of the worldwide e-mail providers like Outlook.com from Microsoft or Gmail from

Google. It is certainly uncommon (although not unheard of) for people to go to much smaller e-mail only or e-mail specialist hosting companies, but to be honest, their piece of the action is being rapidly depleted by the Microsoft's and Googles of the world.

Specifics of DNS hosting

DNS is a bit of a special case when it comes to hosting. As we know it is the very core of the Internet and without it everything stops, however, it is actually a very simple thing for a hosting company to host, generally.

As we know, a DNS server is there to service the incoming requests for a domain name (or part of a domain) and in turn respond with an IP address. It's actually a very simple task and easy for a server to perform, but it comes down to a question of how much control and granularity of control, you need with your DNS records.

Let's take an example of a small business that operates a kind of a directory of other businesses. The entities who choose to list in this directory can avail themselves of an offer to have a pretty standard looking template website created automatically to show their logo and opening hours and a bit of blurb about the entity when they first take out a listing. In order to leverage off the popularity of the host site, the entities listed get themselves a sub-domain address from the hosting site that they are free to market as their own website. So maybe the first registrant will get site1.popularsite.com, the second entity gets site2.popularsite.com and so on. We can see immediately in order make that happen we are going to have to update our DNS record to add our new "A" type entries for each sub-domain as a new registrant comes on board, and to keep our new registrant happy, we rather want their information page (or "website") to be available to the world in short order. We are going to need to have our DNS record with a pretty low TTL to enable that to happen, and we may even need a DNS hosting company who allows us to automatically change our DNS record without having to do the update manually.

This would be the ideal kind of candidate for dedicated DNS hosting because a generic hosting company would likely not allow for a DNS record to have a sufficiently low TTL to enable the updates in a reasonable time, and almost certainly wouldn't have a DNS system that allowed for automated updates.

Of course, this is a very limited kind of requirement: for the most part, DNS records don't change very often. In fact, the vast majority of records haven't changed since the day that the domain name first came into existence, and in those cases there is nothing more needed than the services that can be easily supplied by a generic, general hosting company.

Your needs in this and any other regard may well be different for any number of reasons, and I am not suggesting that these are rules by any means, they are generalities and suggestions; if necessary, you should take proper technical advice specific to your requirements if you think that split DNS (or split any kind of) hosting is the way for your company to go.

Website and e-mail hosting

The public face of your company comes from your website and your e-mail contacts, and this is where you will need to pay some amount of attention when choosing your hosting company. Everyone wants their website to be lightning fast to react to any request, of course they do, and that is the number one request from all customers to hosting companies: can my website be made to go faster please. Choosing the right web hosting company here can actually make a real difference to the way in which a website responds to requests.

There are plenty of other considerations in choosing a web hosting company; not least the type of platform that is required (is it a Windows based website that is being hosted, or does it need a Linux server), is there a database to consider, and so on, but most of this would have already been decided by whoever it was that built your website in the first place, so you'd need to ask them about that; but when it comes to response times there are a couple of key things to bear in mind – some of them your web hosting company has an influence over, some they don't - so let's have a look at the things to think about.

We know from our earlier sections – especially if you were brave enough not to skip over the section on packet switching and routing – that everything on the Internet (in terms of visiting a website at least) comes down to packets of data going back and forth between your web browser and the server upon which the site is ultimately hosted. Those data packets can only travel at a finite speed – it may well be pretty damn quick, but it is nonetheless, finite – and high school mathematics tells us that time taken equals distance to travel divided by speed. Therefore, if the distance to travel back and forth is longer, and the speed is pretty constant, then the time taken to do the trip is higher which means your website takes longer to respond to each request. Therefore, one of the biggest factors in site responsiveness is the distance between your main customer base and the physical location of the server hosting the website. If your client base is in Australia for example, then having your website hosted on servers in Australia will usually result in faster response times than the same server hosted outside of Australia.

As a business owner or manager, this is something over which you have complete control: when selecting a hosting company, either for the first time or when switching, always ask where their servers are physically located and if that is not close to your customer base then seriously consider whether they are the right hosting company for your business. You'll find that around the world there are cheap places to have servers and expensive (comparatively) places to have servers and this will be generally reflected - at least in part – in the prices charged by the company you are looking at.

The next part of the speed puzzle for hosting is the actual server itself. This is completely within the control of the hosting company: servers should be configured correctly, have sufficient resources and not be overloaded by hosting too many websites. If your host has done their job properly then their servers should be regularly maintained, well specified in terms of resources (although they don't have to tell you what those specifications are quite often) and not so laden with sites to host that they are literally crippled by their own workload. Ask a hosting company questions on this subject, and see how they answer you ... see whether they answer you at all.

Finally, the part that is not in the control of the hosting company: your website design. You probably haven't built your website yourself; that would have been done by a specialist company, but if they have built a website that is not working efficiently, then regardless of where it is physically located, and how finely tuned the hosting server, it will still be slow.

They are the keys to website hosting: get those bits right and choose the right hosting company that can help make them right, and not too much will go wrong. E-mail hosting by comparison is a cake walk – that simply comes down to whether or not the hosting company allows you to have the right number of e-mail addresses to suit your business needs, and whether or not they allow the right amount of storage. After that, you're starting to split hairs between companies because there isn't really too much difference between e-mail hosting from company A and company B.

Chapter 8: Websites

My website: It's really all I care about
So, here we are then at chapter eight and we finally get to turn our attention to the first part of the web that people are truly familiar with: websites. Although not ubiquitous in Australia or around the world like they ought to be for businesses of any size, the number of businesses – especially small businesses – with websites displaying their wares, or giving customers the ability to communicate and purchase online is growing every day.

The likelihood is that your business already has a website set up (otherwise, let's be honest: it's unlikely that you would be going through this book) so it is important now to understand how that website fits into the overall scheme of things. We'll discuss a little bit in general terms about how that website works, what it needs in order to run, and where to turn when things go wrong. By the time we are done you should have a pretty decent understanding of what can happen to a website (which almost always involves something going wrong) and have the fear that could have made the hairs on the back of your neck stand up just six chapters ago, replaced with a calm, collected plan of action.

What skills are needed and who do I turn to
Way back in the introduction we talked about our pizza-loving, caffeine-swigging IT guy being the solution to all problems, and the person to whom everyone turns when a situation has anything to do with any appliance connected to a plug. In reality though, the best websites on the web are not really the invention of a single person. There are literally millions of people around the world who can do each role required in creating a website, but that's not to say that they are either

particularly good at any one of them, and they are likely not to be good at all of them. When it comes to the website for a small business, more often than not, the website is either built by the IT guy or by the kid down the road, the child of so-and-so because they are good with computers, says that they just did a website for school, and, let's face it, they were cheap!

Rest assured we, and by that I mean the rest of the world – which includes your current and potential customers – can tell when a website has been built by a kid down the road, so be warned. They stick out like a sore thumb!

Assuming then that your website has been built by a company, let's look at some of the types of people involved in the process and take a look at the roles that they all play.

Essentially websites will be split into three distinct areas – you may have heard the term of a *three-tier architecture* in the past in relation to a software application – as follows:

- Database (sometimes called the backend) – this is where all of your product data or customer information is stored
- Business logic – this is the layer that handles "how" the website works under the covers: it ensures that the correct data comes out of the database, that correct data is written back to the database, and that any calculations and so on are done correctly
- The user interface (often shortened to UI and sometimes known as the frontend) – this is the layer that your users interact with, it contains the text and images and whatever on your site, handles all of what is known as user experience, or UX. Essentially, the only layer of the three that your customers will see.

It should be immediately obvious just from seeing these three layers that the skillsets for each are quite different from each other, and although there are some that overlap (for example, database and business logic can be very similar), they are very different from the UI; the first two require a logically-thinking brain on the part of the developer whereas the UI requires someone with a very creative, imaginative brain.

Generally speaking, those of us who concern ourselves with the "how" a website works (and therefore deal with databases and business logic) are absolutely useless at anything relating to design, and those people who are excellent at design really don't think in a way that databases and business logic components need in order to work properly or efficiently. If you have found yourself someone who can, REALLY can, do all three then you need to be paying that person a lot of money and keeping them locked up as they are as rare as hen's teeth.

This book is not about working out who is, or are, the best person or people to build or maintain your site, but you should be aware of which types of people are best for which "layer" of the site as, at the very least, it will enable you to talk to the right person in the event of a problem.

What you need to know about your website

It's absolutely impossible for any book to know about your website, but it would be a worthwhile discussion to have with your IT guy (if they are still around and not at a Star Wars convention somewhere) or your website developer; at the very least as a business owner or manager you should have an understanding of how your site is put together, which technologies it employs, and have access to all of the relevant parts of it.

Just assuming that your website will work all the time is at best naïve, and at worst a dereliction of your duty as a business owner. You need to know whether your website has a database behind it, if it does, what does that database store (and there are security and compliance implications here too) and which database engine is being used (is it something mainstream like SQL Server, MySQL or Oracle, or is it one of the newer, emerging databases like Mongo DB or something else); you need to know whether the pages are static HTML or whether you use a *Content Management System* (CMS) such as WordPress or Joomla etc., or maybe even a bespoke system for updating your pages, you need to know which language the pages are built in and where the source code for those pages are stored.

This may all seem a little bit dramatic and far too deep of a requirement for a website, but consider the situation where your IT guy has gone, your website has broken and you need it fixed. Now. You are going to need to call in someone to help you, and you can guarantee that after that consultant has listened to your problem, of the first five questions they put to you, the site language, database engine and content management system questions will be three of them. The other two will likely be something like “when do you need it done” and “when do I get paid”.

Static vs. dynamic content

Now that we are starting to peel back the layers of a website a little bit we are beginning to see how each layer interacts with the next; and this steers us quite neatly into the subject of static content vs. dynamic content.

The place to start with this part of the discussion is to define the two phrases: *static content* and *dynamic content*.

A common belief is that every page of a website that is visited has been built like the pages of a book, and is called up on demand and shown, but this is not the case. If this thought is followed through slightly it could not possibly be the case: a book is entirely static – once written and published it is set there forever in black and white, it cannot be changed – whereas the Internet is changing every second, and in many cases as soon as the page is displayed it is out of date (think about a real time stock ticker for example, that will show the price of a stock at a given time). Instead, the majority of pages of websites on the Internet are dynamic, and don't actually exist in a single form at any point, they are built on-the-fly by the web server at the time they are requested.

If you think about your preferred search engine – it cannot have an unlimited number of pages for every conceivable search to begin with; it would be impossible for someone to think in advance of every possible combination of words and phrases that could be searched upon and have a pre-defined set of results available to display. Even an attempt to automate such a task is doomed to failure, and practically impossible to achieve when considering a single language, let alone the hundreds of languages spoken around the world and the way that new words and phrases come into existence almost constantly, and the way that people mix words from different languages in the same text.

This is where your back end website level comes into play – the database. It is from the database that the majority of pages are displayed. A good example would be a product catalogue – your website may host a shopping cart, and you may have some kind of interface to modify the products on sale, which when selected to be available, magically appear on the relevant webpage. What is happening there is that the page selected (the product listing page) is looking up the data from the database – a process called *querying* the database – and is outputting those results in a pre-defined format to build the page. So in reality, the webpage itself is not for the content, but for the rules as to how to display any content that it is given, hence it is dynamic content.

Static content, by contrast is almost exactly like the pages of a book; they have been created once and are served up upon request. The information contained therein doesn't change. Unlike a book, static content can be changed but it is a manual process – someone needs to get in there and change the HTML code over the page to change the information shown. It's not built on-the-fly by the webserver and database at all.

Content management systems and databases

One of the most common ways in which a site is made to be dynamic is through the use of a Content Management System – a phrase that was introduced earlier in this chapter when we were first discussing the various website layers. At the time a few Content Management Systems were cited: WordPress and Joomla.

So what is the purpose of a Content Management System – usually shortened to the initials of just CMS – how does it work in relation to the website that your company is using. This is where the fact that most webpages are just rules for the purposes of displaying information comes into play: the CMS creates those rules, it then allows you to enter the text and other information that you would like to have on your website – the Content part – and the rules as created will take care of how that content actually finds its way onto the page and ultimately, how it looks when displayed.

For example, your CMS may allow you to add a product browser page to your website, and may give the option as to the number of items to display on a page, how many across and down, whether they are displayed in boxes and whether they can be added to a shopping cart etc. Actually, the various possibilities are quite literally limitless as to how a CMS can work because they are usually infinitely flexible in what and how they show. In all cases, the content part of the equation – the text, product names, images, pricing and everything else is stored in the database.

With that in mind, we can now see how the three layers of a website all come together in order to display the page of interest: the database contains the content that we are looking to show, the business logic is responsible for querying the database and extracting the content elements that we would like to show, and the front end uses its display rules to format that output from the business logic layer such that it is attractive and useable to your website user.

And who said that this web stuff was difficult? When you get to have an understanding of the general concepts involved, suddenly the fog starts to lift and the complexity starts to disappear. That's not to say that it is easy because it isn't, although the structures are super simple to understand, the implementation of those structures is the bit that takes all those years of study and experience to get right. An appropriate analogy might be that there are any number of people who know how the internal combustion engine works, they know how everything is connected together and what each part does; but ask them to build a new one from scratch and they very quickly run out of expertise. It's the same with a website: you now know how the bits fit together, but it takes professional, skilled people to take those bits and turn them into something that could be called a useable website.

Getting good search engine rankings

Before we wrap up this topic on how your website might work, we do need to touch on the elephant in the room whenever it comes to building a website: how do you get it onto the first page of "insert name of your favourite search engine" because of course, that's the only way that your online business can succeed. At least, it's what many will have you believe.

As usual with these sorts of things, that phrase rather plays on the lack of knowledge around the subject, and - you'll be completely unsurprised to learn - allows many companies to make profitable businesses out of attempting to get websites onto the first page of a search engine.

If only it were that simple.

Let us quickly dissect the objective for a second before we are able to arrive at some more sensible solutions in a little while. And again, the specifics involved in this process go beyond this introduction to the Internet book, but there are some things worth noting, and there are some myths worth busting.

First of all, can you get to the front page of a search engine? Yes, you can. But will you? Almost certainly not, no. Think about it logically: on most search engines there are about twenty or so results per pages, how many companies just like yours are trying to be one of those twenty? It's reasonable to assume that it is a considerably higher number, so elementary logic tells us that if you have one hundred competitors selling the same widgets as you, then at any time, only twenty of them can be on that much heralded front page. Of course, it's much easier to get to the front page for more obscure search terms, but most people search for generic things which makes the task all that much less likely to be successful.

Secondly, not being on the first page of the search engine will render your web strategy a waste of time, money and effort. That's simply not true: as long as your site is well designed and well built, and meets the needs of your visitors then it will be used whenever people find it. Treat your website like you would your phone number: you wouldn't put out any printed material without your phone number on, and the same should be true of your website.

There are ways to assist your search engine ranking, and there are very reputable companies around who are expert at tailoring websites such that they use those assistances to the best advantage, but there are a couple of things that will absolutely trump anything else you do in regards to getting a decent search ranking. The first is content: if you have a website that always has fresh content, then that website will always rank higher than a website with stale content because it will be seen to be better maintained and meeting the changing needs of the general web surfer.

The second key to the kingdom is inbound links. The more pointers there are on other websites to your own, the more informative a resource your website is considered by the search engines to be, and will therefore rank higher. Be careful here though, get caught using paid inbound link services and the search engine will probably just kick your site out of the search results completely. Do it properly, grow your links organically (as the current phraseology puts it). In other words, try to build your links honestly, by getting links from reputable websites which would – in the normal course of their business – be linking to you anyway. That way you will get good results with no risk of being kicked out of the search results.

Optimising your website for better result ranking is a delicate – and ever changing – balance of science and art. Steer clear of anyone offering a quick fix, and certainly clear of those guaranteeing a first page result – we have just seen that such a guarantee is not possible to fulfil, and besides, it is not in the gift of that company or person to make such a promise. It's very easy to tweak too much and that will lead to worse search result ranking.

The top and bottom of it is that search engine rankings help, there is absolutely no doubt about that, but they are not the be-all and end-all of a web strategy; anyone who thinks otherwise probably ought to be in a different field of work. Just make sure your website is up-to-date (a task that CMSs help with tremendously) and make sure it works properly and meets the needs of your users; if they keep coming back and using it then it will become popular by itself with very little extra help from you.

Chapter 9: E-mail

E-mail: My business is nothing without it
The second main "pillar" of the Internet is undoubtedly e-mail; it's entirely ubiquitous now and for most companies it is absolutely essential, and why wouldn't it be – the ability to have communication in near real time with your customers and suppliers around the world has been an absolute boon that has revolutionised almost every single business on the planet, and created more than a few new ones by its sheer presence.

It's just such a shame that so few people actually know how it works.

Like the other subject matter that we have covered in this book, the idea here is not to dive too deeply into the intricacies of how e-mail works, how it gets from one person to another (although of course we will take a look at it, besides, now you know about DNS you could probably figure the most of it out for yourself anyway), but to give you a decent grounding in the fundamentals such that, at the very least, the terms and phrases don't leave you with a visible question mark above your head, and you are able to understand the various pieces of the e-mail puzzle.

Ask anyone who has used it what their e-mail address is, and assuming they can get the domain name right, they will have a decent stab at coming back with the right answer for you; gone (mostly) are the days when you ask someone for their e-mail address and the response comes back with "www" on the beginning of it. We would pretty much shake our collective heads at that sort of a response now, but back when e-mail was still very new, it was quite common. Ask the same, more e-mail literate people what their mailbox alias is and the look of complete confusion is evident on their face by the time you have finished asking the question.

And here is the main problem with most people's comprehension of e-mail: almost all of the terms used by many have little to no bearing on how these terms are used by people who know how e-mail works, and when you find yourself in trouble because your e-mail isn't working, it is to these people that you will likely find yourself talking, so it would be a good idea to be talking mostly the same sort of language. If the thought currently trundling through your brain goes along the lines of: how could this possibly be important, everyone knows what an e-mail address is, then take a second to stop and think about the sorts of people with whom you will be dealing when your orders are no longer coming in on the sales e-mail account, and your sales manager is busily jumping up and down in front of your desk, sweat gushing from every pore, and furrow lines on their forehead deepening so quickly that you can sit there and watch it happen. The people on the other end of the phone, let's be honest, are going to be geeks. Of course it is a massive generalisation to tar them all with the same brush, but if you want to get into a conversation about the merits of the use of seven decimal places of Pi rather than the usual four, then it's probably fair to say that it would be in the general direction of a geek that you will be heading. The underlying point here is that geeks, and computer geeks in particular, tend to use the language of the computer rather than the language of the person when speaking, even on the rare occasions that they speak to a person. Therefore, if like most people, you don't speak geek, it's quite easy to get off on the wrong foot; quite easy for both parties to become very annoyed with each other and quite easy for your phone conversation to degenerate from the exchange of words to the dreaded monotone buzz of a terminated call.

For the sake of your business, and the general health and wellbeing of your now completely exhausted sales manager, having the ability to translate to and from Geek-speak is a useful skill to have. Being able to speak in the same terms as your neighbourhood geek or the phone-based geek, upon whom you, in your hour of need, so completely depend, will mean that you are more likely to get the help you need than to be given the brush-off as just another person who knows absolutely nothing about anything, ever.

Let's start then with a quick review of some common vocabulary that you are going to run into almost immediately when the aforementioned geek begins their utterances - almost none of which you would have likely encountered in your day to day life, but to those people handling e-mail, it is the de facto parlance.

We all know what an e-mail address is: essentially, somebody @ some domain. The domain part we already know about because we went through that in some detail earlier in the book, so now that bit is easy.

The part of the e-mail address preceding the "at" is known as the *alias* (or sometimes, *e-mail alias*) which at first seems like an odd choice of word for it, surely it would be better as "the name" or "the person" or something.

Well yes, that may well be the case, but that wouldn't really be an accurate description of the realities of use: there are many times when an alias is used by a department for example, so not a person at all … think about reception@ for example. Or, it may be a generic term, like help@ a domain or the more common info@. That's why this is known as an alias: it is an alternate name for an anything. For the remainder of this chapter, I will refer to the initial part of an e-mail address (the part before the "@" symbol) as the alias.

Most people would be of the belief that when they send an e-mail to an address, it will arrive with a person, and for the most part that is true but in reality there are three types (for want of a better phrase) of end points to an e-mail address:

The main one that will be encountered is a *mailbox.* A mailbox is used in exactly the way you would expect it to be; the same way that your mailbox at home works. It's where the e-mail messages actually end up, in the same way that your postal mail ends up in your mailbox at home. All e-mail messages must end up somewhere (assuming that they are correctly addressed of course), that may be a single mailbox if we have addressed an e-mail to person@ domain, or it could be a shared mailbox perhaps in our instance of reception@ domain, or it could be any number of mailboxes if an alias refers to a group of people, maybe in the example of info@ domain – that message could be farmed out to dozens of individual mailboxes.

Before we go on here, and this is just an aside, when an e-mail message is sent to multiple mailboxes such as our example of info@ domain, the message isn't actually initially duplicated that many times wasting storage space, it's a bit of an illusion really but works rather well - at least well enough to have people believe they each get a copy of the mail message, which they don't. All of that intelligence is dealt with by the mail server.

Back to our current topic though, and we have started off with the simplest of e-mail types with the mailbox, but we have also already touched on the other two.

The second to look at is an *e-mail group* (or list): this is our info@ domain – the e-mail alias (info) actually goes to a number of specified mailboxes. It's as simple as that, no tricks to it.

The third and final type is an alias: an alternate name for a mailbox. This is used in the situation where a person may have their own mailbox (jsmith@ domain), but they would prefer that people got into the habit of e-mailing reception@ domain, so that in the event that user using the jsmith mailbox either leaves the company, or at least is no longer responsible for reception duties, then the new receptionist who has their own mailbox (bdoe@ domain) can come into the role without the need for customers to be informed of the change and start sending to a new e-mail address.

For your e-mail addresses that are currently in use, all of the above would have been configured by your IT guy initially, but if that person has left the company then you are likely going to find yourself in the position of having to administer mail for existing and new employees at some stage; it is then that you may find yourself staring down the barrel of an e-mail configuration control panel with your hosting company, and will find that all of the above words and phrases will be used. At least now you will understand what it is that you are being asked.

Who looks after my e-mail

Talking of hosting companies, let's take a look at where all of the e-mail that travels around actually ends up: with all of these e-mail messages bouncing around the place – and there are billions of them every second of every day going around (most of them are spam actually, but we'll get on to that in a minute), someone has to deal with them and look after those messages, so where do they all end up? Does your company have a disk somewhere with these messages sitting on it or what?

Well, as with everything IT, the honest answer is that it depends. As usual, there are any number of solutions to a single problem, and although your company will employ one of them (it has to), which one is chosen would have been a business decision taken some time ago, and quite likely by someone other than you. As seems to be common in what we have been looking at, there are three possibilities as to where your e-mail actually – I would say physically, but that's rather a misnomer as it's not really a physical item – lives.

The first option for e-mail is what is called *On-premise hosting*, and I mention it first because for small businesses it is the most unlikely scenario which means we can skip over it quickly. On premise hosting requires that you have a decided mail server in your office or at your data centre, and they often require a reasonable amount of care and attention to maintain. Although in the longer term it can be a cost effective solution for larger businesses, for a small business it is just too expensive in terms of equipment and man power to use. So on premise hosting is an option, but beyond that we shall not discuss it as given you are reading this book, it is unlikely to be relevant to you.

The second e-mail option is the one which the majority of small businesses currently find themselves using. That is that their e-mail is based upon a *hosted e-mail service*, usually – for the sake of convenience, simplicity and practicality for the most part – that would be with the same company that hosts the website for you. Almost all web hosting companies will offer some kind of e-mail hosting facilities too. As I said, this is the most popular option so if you have trouble with your e-mail then your most likely first port of call will be your web hosting company.

The final option is very similar to having your e-mail with your web hosting provider, but instead, it will be with one of the large multinational companies. Names that spring to mind immediately would be Outlook.com (formerly known as Hotmail) from Microsoft, and Gmail or Yahoo to name but three. There are any number of them around the world. Some small businesses have their e-mail hosted with these companies because often it is free although naturally, there are paid versions of these services that all of those companies will offer. This option – which doesn't really have a name of its own, but I shall refer to as *Global e-mail hosting* - is separate from the hosted e-mail service purely because it is provided by a supplier other than that which looks after your website hosting.

Of course, there are pluses and minuses to each of these solutions, and which one suits you is something that only you can know. Generally speaking, if you are stuck as to which to select, you should always play safe and host your e-mail with the same company that does your website hosting; it can always be changed later on anyway ... as we know from our discussions on DNS records, it's really only changing of the MX entry in your DNS record that determines who hosts your e-mail.

Given that we could now take a reasonable stab at figuring out where our mail is held, we need to get into the realms of which type of e-mail is being hosted.

Initially this may seem like an odd question as there is really only one type of e-mail message, but the type of e-mail account that has been configured can have a profound effect on whether or not your hosting company are going to be able to help you out at all, and where the mail message currently lives (which is useful if it needs to be recovered after having been accidentally deleted for example).

When it comes to types of e-mail account – and for the purposes of this part of the book I am assuming that the e-mail is being hosted for you, either by your hosting company or by a global host, (this doesn't apply to those of you with on premises e-mail hosting) – there are two distinct types of e-mail account, you may even have heard the terms for them before too. They are *POP* (sometimes known as *POP3* in deference to the beginnings of this standard) which stands for Post Office Protocol, and *IMAP* (Internet Mail Access Protocol). Under the covers these are called protocols; we have spoken briefly about protocols previously when we were examining the structure of a domain name, and it was mentioned that the protocols there were http or https, and were used to indicate how the communications were to take place. The same is true of POP and IMAP, the protocol determines how the e-mail exchange between your computer and the hosting company is to be conducted.

The protocol conversation is largely irrelevant for the most part as they tend to just work and that's all you need to know, but there is a VERY big difference as to how the mail is treated for each type of protocol, and it is imperative that you are able to know the difference between the two and what each means for your business.

The difference relates to where an e-mail message is stored at the time that it appears in your inbox. With an e-mail account configured for use by the POP (or POP3) protocol, that mail message is downloaded from the hosting company's mail server onto whatever machine you are using to access your inbox. In the case of IMAP, the message stays on the hosting company's server and your inbox (and other mail folders) are synchronised to it.

As with everything, there are helpful and unhelpful aspects to each type of protocol and which one you choose depends upon your personal and business requirements.

Let's look first at the IMAP protocol as just now, that is the more popular of the two.

As I mentioned before, accounts configured for IMAP store all of the mail on the hosting company's servers, and this means that your inbox is merely a window into the contents of the mailbox that they maintain for you.

IMAP periodically synchronises the mail and folders between your computer and the hosting company's server, so if you move an e-mail between folders locally on your machine, that move will be replicated at the next synchronisation. Likewise, if you delete the message, it will be deleted from the servers too.

IMAP is very useful if you use multiple computers and devices to access your inbox, they will all be synchronised all the time, meaning that looking at your inbox from your laptop will look the same as looking at it from your phone, without the need for you to do anything special. The hazard of course is that if you accidentally delete that message from your inbox on your phone, that delete will be replicated across all devices.

POP by contrast does not synchronise with the mail server at all, instead, it will periodically poll the mail server with the question "do you have anything new to show me?" If there is, the new mail message is downloaded to the machine or device that you are using, and marked on the server as having been downloaded. That means that if you were to refresh your mailbox (commonly referred to as send/receive as that is the terminology used by Microsoft Outlook) on your laptop and three new e-mails were there, they would be downloaded to your laptop. If you were to then do the same from your phone, it would not receive any new messages because they have been marked as already having been received.

With POP, the mail messages are stored on the device that downloads them, not on the hosting company's servers, so your devices will not be automatically synchronised and each device may have a different view of the mailbox at any given time.

Of course, there are tricks that can be done with POP to make this a little easier for use on multiple devices because it does support an option to not mark an e-mail as having been downloaded in some situations which can enable this functionality, but it is a little complicated and prone to error if not configured properly.

With so many people accessing e-mail on multiple devices now it is easy to see why IMAP is quickly becoming the standard, but as I have mentioned just now, it needs to be treated with respect because computers have a habit of doing what you tell them to, rather than what you want them to do, and that extends to "delete all of my e-mail please". So tread carefully.

Configuration requirements for e-mail accounts

Having now looked through what POP and IMAP e-mail accounts are, there may be a vague memory of some of the terms trying to make its presence felt in the back of your head, and that thought may be trying to remind you of the time that you had to configure your e-mail account on a new laptop or on the phone, and you may well be recalling an image of the page of e-mail configuration options on your e-mail client of choice that previously would have resulted in sighs of utter despair and confusion, because that all-too-common configuration dialogue asks about such things. If you were to go back and look at that screen of e-mail configuration options now, it would all of a sudden be considerably clearer. That is until you are prompted to enter server addresses because knowing what you know now, you may ask yourself why that is even required if everything is dealt with via the DNS record.

Well, this is where we introduce a third protocol into the mix ... shocker. It always turns out that these things come in threes doesn't it?

You'll notice that when we were talking about POP and IMAP, we were talking about receiving e-mail and synchronising and all that sort of thing, what we didn't mention was sending of e-mail. That's where the third protocol makes its presence felt: it's a protocol called *SMTP* (Simple Mail Transfer (or Transport)

Protocol) and its job is to handle the sending of e-mails from your mailbox to wherever they are going.

So we have one outbound protocol (SMTP) and one of two inbound protocols (POP or IMAP) to deal with, and this is one of the reasons that the configuration dialogue looks so daunting, it needs to be told all of this information in order for your e-mail to flow.

But why do we need to furnish the computer with this information, does the DNS not contain such information in the MX record?

Well no, sadly. The DNS record doesn't tell the world anything about the servers used for sending of e-mail, it just tells Internet users looking to send e-mail to you where that message ought to be sent. One reason for this is all to do with the prevention of sending of SPAM; in order for a mail server to be considered less likely to be sending SPAM, that server needs to be specifically identified to the Internet as being a mail server, this is done by a process called *Reverse DNS* (often shortened to rDNS) which is the exact oppose of the DNS that we have looked at previously. In our look at DNS we were taking a domain name and turning it into an IP address so that our address can be routed, but in the header of an e-mail message that is sent there is a reference not only to the IP address of the sending server, but to the domain name of that sending server. What a receiving mail server will do is to do a reverse DNS lookup of the IP address supplied to see whether it matches the domain name supplied in the e-mail header. If it does, then the message is more likely to be legitimate, if it doesn't then there is a pretty fair chance that it is SPAM. Whether or not it is considered to be SPAM is in part controlled by a record in your DNS entry with a TXT type which specifies rules relating to a system called the *Sender Policy Framework* (SPF) which essentially says "which IP addresses can an e-mail come from and it still be considered to be from me"; this can go a little way to preventing your domain being used by a spammer because they will usually not use one of your IP addresses when sending their mail out.

Any way around, we cannot rely upon our DNS record to provide the SMTP server address for us, so we must do that ourselves. Normally your hosting provider will give you all of the server addresses that you are going to need so if in doubt, contact them, but it should now start to be coming a little clearer as to where you might want to look if you start to have e-mail problems. For example, if you can receive e-mail but not send, then we can assume that there is going to be a problem with the server that has been specified for our outbound protocol – our SMTP server. If the opposite is true and we can send, but not receive then the finger of suspicions points initially to our POP or IMAP server.

See, it's not rocket science, and it's actually not all that tricky to work out; all you need is someone to point you in the right direction to begin with.

Do I have a backup in case it gets deleted?
This discussion leads us to the obvious question of: is my e-mail backed up in case I (or someone) makes a complete rickets of it, and deletes the whole lot?

You're probably already able to pre-empt the answer actually: if you have an IMAP account then the chances are that your hosting company will have a backup of the e-mail messages but it will likely not be as of five minutes ago; it is at best going to be the state of play overnight as most hosting companies will back up their mail servers nightly. If you don't have a great hosting company then they may only back up their mail servers once a week, and may not even do it at all. Just because they have a backup though, doesn't mean you'll be able to get your hands on it – most hosting companies back up their servers using images (basically a snapshot of the server at a point in time) which is different to the way most consumer backup systems work, they essentially take copies of files, whereas the server image takes a copy of the entire server. Server images are a great way to back up lots of data in a short space of time, but they are not useful for recovering individual files, or, as in this case, the lost mailbox. They are used for restoring entire servers to a known-good state when they fall into a pile of smouldering resistors and memory chips. Therefore, although your hosting company may well hold a backup of your deleted mailbox, in order to get it back, they are going to have to restore the entire server to somewhere, then go get your mailbox from that new server and copy it to your mail location before throwing that restore away. It can be done, but you will absolutely be charged for the privilege of them doing it for you, so be careful.

With POP, your hosting company will not have a copy of the e-mail, so don't rely upon them.

In all instances, it is always best to assume that you are responsible for backing up your e-mail if it is that important to your business, and therefore should employ whatever strategy is required to ensure that should the worst happen, you can recover.

E-mail security

When we look around the web we can tell how secure or otherwise our connection to the current website either is or isn't by the presence or otherwise of the tell-tale padlock somewhere on the screen, and the https protocol indicator in the address bar. But what about e-mail? Is that covered by the same kind of protection? Is the content of the e-mail that I am sending to a colleague safe and secure whilst in transit or at its destination?

Put simply, the answer is no. E-mail by default is an entirely insecure mechanism of data transport; much like sending a postcard through the mail – anyone who sees it along the way can read the content of the message in clear text (or unencrypted) for the most part.

This is beginning to change slowly, but really only in part. If you have access to your mailbox over the web then in all likelihood you will connect to that server over an https connection meaning that the connection between your device and the server is secure, and that's a great start. If you don't have, or don't use, web-based e-mail then some providers do offer the same sort of connection from your e-mail client (like Microsoft Outlook) to the server, using the equivalent of an https connection called a connection over SSL (Secure Sockets Layer), and yes, that is the same SSL that the https connection is based upon.

Of course, this is great for the connection between your device and the mail server, but what about when the mail is being sent between your SMTP server and the server specified by the recipients' MX entry, is that secure?

The safest approach by far is to say no, unfortunately. No amount of https or SSL connection to your SMTP server can guarantee that the inter-server communication is safe, and this is a weakness in the current architecture of e-mail. If any server along the route (and if you read the chapter on packet switching then you'll know that there could be any number of servers and switches involved along the way) chose to, it could read and store those data packets passing through it, and recompile them into a copy of the message that is being sent – it's a process called a "*Man in the Middle*" (or MITM) attack.

I very much doubt that most users of e-mail are aware of just how trivially easy it is to read e-mail whilst in transit; I think because the default icon for e-mail is a letter in an envelope that they believe that the surrounding envelope protects the contents, in the same way that an envelope going through the postal system would.

There are ways to mitigate against this inherent weakness by employing tools for encrypting e-mail, but currently they are very cumbersome to use, and almost nobody uses them which makes them even more complicated because each sender/recipient pair must first exchange encryption/decryption keys and it just makes the whole process very painful.

I guess that's why even after decades in this business, I still shake my head whenever I see someone sending their credit card details in an e-mail. They wouldn't send cash through the mail, but credit card details in the e-mail message seems to be totally secure to them. Please don't be one of those people.

Despite its insecurity there is still much e-mail that is sent, and knowing what we have now learned in this chapter, we get to the real purpose of our discussion. It may not have been obvious at the beginning, and to be fair, I didn't actually set out at the beginning of the chapter what it was that we would be heading towards, but nevertheless, here we are. And what we are going to be looking at for the final, enthralling episode of all things e-mail, is bounce messages.

Cue the groans of disappointment, I know, but actually, there is a point to it, and everything that I have talked about thus far does actually naturally lead to this point.

The first sign that most people get to indicate that all is not well with their mail system, is when the dreaded message from "System Administrator" comes back advising that the carefully crafted e-mail to great aunt Dorothy - who you have been meaning to write to for the past six months, honestly! - did not get delivered, and your well-chosen and heartfelt words were never received because they went no further than some faceless server, and now find themselves back in your inbox. Bugger.

The problem with these *non-delivery reports* (called either NDR, or more commonly, bounce messages) is that they start off innocently enough with a gentle note saying something like "we're terribly sorry, but we couldn't deliver your message" (no mention of who we are of course), but then goes on in a very much less gentle tone to describe to you just how it wasn't able to be delivered using a stream of absolute garbage text which may as well be a Klingon representation of Egyptian hieroglyphics, and is therefore largely unintelligible.

That is until you had been through this chapter. If you were to take another look at a bounce message now, it wouldn't be anywhere near as cryptic as it was before: it'll be talking about SMTP servers – you know about them now, the technical term for a sending mail server - it will be talking (possibly) about DNS records that you know about already, mailbox aliases which we have just been talking about, domain names and IP addresses that we have discussed in earlier chapters. Suddenly, it's not as scary as it was.

Now I wouldn't recommend rolling up the sleeves and trying to decode the entire message just yet; although I have little doubt that you would now be able to take a pretty decent stab at what it means, and I reckon you'd do a reasonable job of understanding where the problem might lie, but what is still to learn is what this information actually means.

What you need to be aware of is that an NDR although usually bad, is not always completely fatal for your hand crafted missive to Aunty Dot. Remember that the R in NDR is report, it's trying let you know something unusual has happened, you can do with that information what you choose.

The question then becomes, what to choose?

In every one of these messages – when you know how to ignore the guff and pick out the important bits – there is something that tells you what went wrong, usually in pretty straightforward text. That will be something like “mailbox unavailable”, “mailbox over quota”, “domain not found” or whatever it will be, and that text will often have a code preceding it; those codes will start with 4 or 5 (usually) and will be [number][dot][number][dot][number] (5.1.1 for example). This sequence is a standardised error code which, if you chose to, you could look up on the web for more information. Generally, those codes with a five at the beginning are an error of some kind, those with a four at the beginning are an advice of some description, and indicate that the problem is likely to be temporary and may well resolve itself.

It’s at this point that we add two new terms to our lexicon: *soft bounce* and *hard bounce*, so let’s get into those a bit.

We’ll start with soft bounce as this is the friendlier of the two and a way to ease us into deciphering these messages. A soft bounce indicates that although something has gone wrong with this message delivery, it’s a temporary problem and may well resolve itself in due course, and is basically an advisory to suggest that the message you sent hasn’t arrived, but that’s not necessarily to say that it won’t arrive if you were to send it again.

Let’s take a little detour here into how e-mail servers talk to each other and what they talk about because there is a defined set of rules and responses. We’re not going to go through it in detail, but in brief it looks a bit like this:

We have two servers involved: the sender and the recipient, and we assume that all of the necessary DNS lookups have been done, and we are talking to the correct server based upon its MX entry for the recipient.

- Sender asks the recipient to confirm whether they are responsible for a given domain
- Yes, I am, comes back the response
- Good, can I send you some e-mail, this is who I am
- OK, you look like a server that I am allowed to talk to, who would you like to send to
- I would like to send to info@ domain, is that OK?
- Now here we can get a few answers: either, yes, I know that alias so please start sending. Alternatively, we may get sorry, I don't know that alias – at which point the communication is dropped, rather abruptly actually. The third option is: yes, I know that alias, but I cannot deal with your send request at the moment, please try again later

Increasingly nowadays a receiving server will not confirm nor deny the validity of the e-mail alias at this point as to do so could pose a security risk – something called enumeration. The process of enumeration means to cycle through a list of possible answers to establish whether they are correct. By using this enumeration method on a server that confirms that an alias is valid or invalid, starting at "A" and looping through to "ZZZZZ" @domain will result in all of the valid aliases being obtained. In an effort to prevent this, often the e-mail will be accepted for processing as the domain name is valid, and internal anti-SPAM and anti-malware routines will handle the incoming message, which may well be just deleting it.

We can see from this very simplified (although quite accurate) message exchange that we have the possibility of a transient or temporary condition in place at the recipient's end that prevents the message from being sent, but we also see that there is a mechanism to deal with it: the request to send the message later on.

Mail servers have built into their software a number of what are called *retry intervals*; the number and duration of those intervals is at the behest of the company running the sending server, but they will increase as we go through them. So, the first retry interval may well be five minutes, the second interval may be fifteen minutes, then an hour, then four hours, twelve hours, a day or two days.

Generally, a mail message that cannot initially be sent will be waiting in the send queue for about three or four days, at which time, an NDR will come back advising that the sending server has rather given up now and are bouncing the message completely.

What then would be an example of a soft bounce - how can a recipient server have a temporary problem? Soft bounces are often related to the account status of the recipient; for example: they may have a maximum limit on the amount of mail that could be stored on their account and they may be in excess of that at the time of attempted delivery, the message is therefore soft bounced for retry later to give the recipient time to free up space. Alternatively, the recipient mail server may be up, but not in a position to process mail at the moment. Perhaps it is undergoing maintenance or something.

So simply, soft bounce is advising that the condition currently in place that prevents the delivery of the message is something that may well be fixed in time, and you are welcome to attempt to send the message again later on.

The other end of the spectrum is what is known as a hard bounce, indicated by our error code with 5 [dot] [something] at the beginning. This is something that is not going to be fixed with the passage of time and therefore, re-delivery of the message should not be attempted.

By far the most common of these hard bounces is 5.5.0 (sometimes a 5.5.1) – bad address. The text that the server sends back will likely be different but essentially it's an incorrect recipient mailbox address ... the alias (the part of the address preceding the @ sign) is wrong. Exactly the same as a return to sender, address unknown problem with the postal system.

Hard bounces are permanent (in the context of this e-mail delivery attempt) and the sending servers will not usually go around the retry loop. Your send has failed completely, and you'll need to find out why.

There is nothing that you, as the sender, can do about hard bounces – it could be that the recipients DNS record is missing or out of date or something, which is outside of your control, but you'll only know the extent of the problem by reading the bounce message – something that should now prove to be considerably easier than it would have been previously, now that you are armed with the knowledge and vocabulary to get you to the answer.

What we haven't spoken about here, besides mentioning the term in passing, is SPAM mail. SPAM is the scourge of all mail server administrators and an absolute pain. Essentially SPAM is the automated sending of millions of e-mails to people who have no interest in receiving those e-mails, advising them of things that are of (usually) no interest.

In the earlier days of e-mail these SPAM messages were trying to sell illegal drugs or to boost the price of a particular penny share on some stock market around the world before the original owners offload their holding for a profit (the so-called Pump-and-Dump scheme). From there it moved onto ways to extract money by deception, usually involving some long-lost relative of yours (who you had no idea existed) that was killed in some accident and by absolute chance was in the process of moving millions of dollars around the world, and as the only surviving relative, only you can help – it will cost you your bank details and thousands in "fees" but honestly, you'll get millions in return. Yeah, right! That is called the Nigerian 419 scam – mostly because the perpetrators were originally based in Nigeria and 419 was the police code for such things.

Nowadays, SPAM is much more devious than that: carefully crafted and authentic-looking e-mails arrive (unsolicited) from what purports to be a reputable company with whom you may or may not have dealings, advising you that your account has been locked and you are required to sign in again, all you have to do is follow the link below, blah, blah ... Of course the link is not going to take you to the website of a reputable company, but instead someone posing as that company who will record the details you enter for their own use later on.

All of these don't even mention that SPAM messages are a great attack vector for passing viruses around the web. Who can resist clicking on a link to watch some fun video or another, only to find that the video link was actually a link to some executable file that ran on the machine and it's too late. The virus is now on your machine!

It is for that very reason that almost all operating systems will generate those "annoying" pop-up warnings, telling you that what you are about to do is potentially dangerous. Of course, because people are so bored of seeing those messages they just click "allow", thereby completely negating their usefulness. There is actually a direct correlation between the people who blindly ignore the warning and click allow, with the people who look forlorn and woe-is-me, when they find out that some nefarious person has cleared out their life-savings using the credentials obtained by the key-logged that was “allowed” to run despite the warnings. Do try not to be one of those people!

At the time of writing there is a SPAM e-mail based attack prevalent in the world whereby clicking the link or opening the “invoice” attachment actually runs an application which encrypts the content of the machine which can only then be decrypted by payment of Bitcoin to some address or another.

Luckily, thanks in part to more user awareness, but mostly by huge strides forward in the anti-spam technologies that e-mail providers employ (mostly completely unseen by the user), the levels of SPAM on the Internet is actually starting to decrease, slightly. It is still a huge problem and will continue to be, but will become less of a problem over time.

So that’s what SPAM is, but how does it work and how can we stop it?

SPAM is automated, and is generally not targeted at the recipient; there are servers around the world that continually probe IP addresses looking to see what kind of a response they elicit. That may be a website (for the most part), in which case they will crawl around it looking for e-mail addresses to harvest; or it may be a mail server, in which case that automated tool will fire requests at that server in an effort to convince it to send mail on its behalf (another reason why On-premise e-mail is only for the bravest of companies – imagine trying to counter that threat every second of every day). If successful in convincing the mail server to send mail on its behalf, millions of e-mail messages will be sent to e-mail addresses harvested from the web crawling process; this sending of e-mail will continue until the mail server stops allowing it to happen.

What you, as the owner or manager of small business, can do to prevent SPAM from being used is quite limited. All you can do is to ensure that your staff are educated so as to not follow random links or open random attachments to e-mails, regardless of how authentic they appear, and secondly, make sure that your e-mails are being handled by a company that has the proper infrastructure in place to deal with it correctly, to make sure that their mail servers don't allow spammers to send their messages (these servers are called *Open Relays*, and it wouldn't be a stretch to suggest that whenever a small business runs their own mail server, at some point, albeit completely by accident, one of their mail servers will become an open relay).

What you can do though, is to secure your DNS entries to limit how mail can be sent using your domain name. If you've ever come into the office to find that you have thousands of NDRs in your inbox, then that would be a sign that a spammer has used your domain name (entirely at random usually) to send SPAM messages and appear more legitimate. If that has happened to you, then you probably found that your e-mail host blocked you from using their services at that time too!

If you were to turn back to the section on DNS records, you will notice in the example DNS record shown that there is a TXT type entry in there with a value of: "v=spf1 a mx -all". On the face of it, complete gibberish, but this single line here is a very important step in the fight against SPAM. This is your SPF entry, and it tells mail servers a little bit about how to deal with mail that purportedly comes from your domain name. The syntax of the line is largely irrelevant but if translated says "consider e-mail to be legitimately from my domain if the IP address of the sending mail server is either my website, my global IP address (A) or the IP address of my mail server (MX), if not, consider it to be fraudulent (-all)". With this one little line, a receiving e-mail server can have a good go at knowing whether or not the e-mail being sent from your domain is SPAM or real mail.

You can now consider yourself to be fairly knowledgeable on how e-mail actually works and what you can do in your small way to make it safer for everyone. More importantly, when it stops working or doesn't work as you would like it to, you now at least have a starting point for your diagnostics and eventual resolution to the problem.

A fun factoid for you: using the word SPAM to describe junk messages derives from a comedy sketch from Monty Python's Flying Circus in around 1970. In the skit which was based in a cafe, almost all of the items on the menu were in one way or another, Spam (the tinned luncheon meat product); on occasion, upon mention the word spam, a group of Vikings in the cafe would chant the word SPAM repeatedly, thereby drowning out all other conversation until they were finally told to shut up.

When the Internet first started being used for bulletin boards etc., users coined the term SPAM to describe off-topic and unrelated messages that were posted incessantly to drown out legitimate postings to the board in deference to the sketch. Therefore, when junk e-mail messages became so prevalent on the Internet when e-mail started to be used, it was thus described.

The Monty Python sketch is available online and for the three and a half minutes it runs for, is well worth a viewing and does show that the terminology is quite apt.

Chapter 10: Conclusion

And here we are, we've reached the end of this introductory journey into how the Internet works; hopefully your knowledge has been enhanced as a result of it, and more importantly, that it is no longer some magical black box of jargon that is impenetrable to non-Klingon speakers. Hopefully you can see that everything is actually quite simple when it is broken down into small, easy-to-digest chunks of information and really not all that scary.

Of course this is an introduction, you wouldn't be able to get yourself a PhD with the information in this book but you would at least be able to hold your own when talking to those of us with a techie persuasion as you will inevitably have to in your day-to-day working life. It's possible that this scratching of the surface of knowledge has sparked a bit of an interest in learning more about the subject, and if that's the case then that is wonderful. There are heaps of resources available out there which will take you all the way to that PhD if that's what you want, but it all starts with a single first step, and it looks like this book may have been just that. Enjoy the journey.

I hope that you have enjoyed the book, I hope that you have learned something and maybe reduced some of the fears that could arise from the nightmare scenario of your IT guy running off into the sunset for a larger pay packet somewhere else, and leaving you with that one side of A4 that I alluded to right at the beginning.

At the very least, you'll have hopefully learned about how the Internet all fits together – in summary if not in too much detail.

###

Appendix A: Hosting checklist

With the potential for many hosting accounts for each service that you use, it can be difficult to keep track of which company is hosting which service(s) for you, and the important information you may need for each. Use these checklists to help you keep track of it all.

Website information

Developer's name: ____________________

Contact number: ____________________

E-mail address: ____________________

Technologies in use: ____________________

____

CMS name (if applicable): ____________________

E-mail information

SMTP server address: ____________________

Protocol: POP / IMAP

Backup location(s): ____________________

Hosting information

Website hosting company: ____________________

Phone number: ____________________

E-mail address: ____________________

E-mail hosting company: ____________________

Phone number: ____________________

E-mail address: ____________________

DNS hosting company: ____________________

Phone number: ____________________

E-mail address: ____________________

Other information

Company Internet Service Provider (ISP): ____________

Phone number: ____________________

E-mail address: ____________________

Appendix B: Domain checklist

Having your domain name expire and the lights go out is one of the worst events that can occur to a small business with an online presence. Use the domain checklist below to keep track of your important domain name information.

Domain name: ______________________________

Reseller name: ______________________________

Expiry date:________________________________

Administrative contact: ________________________

Domain name: ______________________________

Reseller name: ______________________________

Expiry date:________________________________

Administrative contact: ________________________

Domain name: ______________________________

Reseller name: ______________________________

Expiry date:________________________________

Administrative contact: ________________________

Domain name: ______________________________

Reseller name: ______________________________

Expiry date: ______________________________________

Administrative contact: ____________________________

Domain name: ___________________________________

Reseller name: __________________________________

Expiry date: ______________________________________

Administrative contact: ____________________________

Domain name: ___________________________________

Reseller name: __________________________________

Expiry date: ______________________________________

Administrative contact: ____________________________

Domain name: ___________________________________

Reseller name: __________________________________

Expiry date: ______________________________________

Administrative contact: ____________________________

Glossary of terms

Alias / e-mail alias

The part of an e-mail address that precedes the "@" symbol and the domain name.

Bit

The smallest amount of information that a computer can store, being either a 1 (true) or 0 (false)

Binary

The system of counting in use by computers, consisting of zeros and ones only

Byte

A collection of 8 bits used by a computer to represent what we would know as a letter, in binary format.

Canonical Name Record

Full name for a CNAME entry in a DNS record, essentially a DNS alias to another domain name.

Content Management System (CMS)

A flexible website display mechanism which allows for page content to be stored in a database as opposed to fixed files, thus allowing web-based content to be changed easily using easy-to-use tools with no specialist web design and coding knowledge

DNS - Domain Name System (or Service)

Routing information for a domain name, analogous to a phonebook in our world. It translates the domain names that we understand into the IP addresses that the Internet works with.

DNS Entry

Single line item of a DNS record

DNS Record

Complete information as to the location (and other useful information) for elements of a domain name.

Domain name

A rented, globally unique, human readable identifier for Internet-based data. Often chosen to match or closely resemble a company name or tagline

Dotted quad

Alternate name for the formatting of an IP address, being four sets of numbers separated by a dot (period)

Dynamic content

Website page information that it retrieved on-the-fly and displayed to the user. An example would be a stock market ticker, or hotel room availability grid

Gigabyte

One Thousand Million (10^9 or 1,000,000,000) bytes

Global e-mail hosting

A phrase used in this book to identify hosting of one's e-mail services with a global player such as Gmail or Outlook.com

Group (e-mail)

An e-mail alias that points to more than one mailbox

Hard bounce

The report of a failed sending of an e-mail message that indicates that the situation is irrecoverable and will not be re-attempted.

Hexadecimal notation

Counting in base-16, being 0-9 + A-F

Hosted e-mail service

The hosting of one's e-mail services with a company specifically providing those services rather than hosting one's own e-mail services On-Premise.

IMAP (Internet Mail Access Protocol)

An e-mail protocol which keeps mail messages on the hosting server and synchronises them to the client device (as opposed to POP/POP3 which downloads and stores the messages locally)

IP Address

Unique numeric location of a server (or group of servers) on the Internet. Written as four groups of numbers ranging 0-255 separated by dots

Interface (routing)

Inbound or outbound connection of a router

Internet Protocol (IP)

The underlying transport mechanism of the Internet, it determines "how" data packets are sent between servers and routers.

Internet Service Provider (ISP)

The company from whom you rent your access to the Internet

Kilobyte

1,000 bytes

Mail Exchanger (MX)

A type of DNS entry specifically for detailing the location of receiving mail servers for a given domain name

Mailbox

Actual location (per e-mail alias) that e-mail messages are stored

Man in the Middle (MITM)

An attack method whereby a nefarious party sits between sender and receiver pretending to be the receiver. The MITM will receive all information sent from the sender, store a copy and send it on to the real receiver, thereby masking its presence. It is a way in which data can be intercepted and used in ways for which it wasn't intended.

Megabyte

One million (10^6 or 1,000,000) bytes

Name server

The authoritative server for DNS queries

Non-Delivery Report (NDR)

Notification to the sender of an e-mail message that either could not be delivered or which has been delayed

Octets

Name for one of the four parts of an IP address

On-premise hosting

The process of hosting one's e-mail (or other resources) in house rather than using a dedicated hosting company

Open Relay

A mail server that has not been correctly secured and locked down which can be exploited for the purposes of sending SPAM

POP/POP3 (Post Office Protocol)

An e-mail protocol whereby mail is downloaded to the client's device rather than being stored on the hosting server and synchronised to (see IMAP for the latter)

Packet

The smallest chunk of data that is sent over the Internet

Packet switching

The process of routing packets around the Internet as quickly as possible utilising numerous routes to the destination

Port

A numbered channel between sender and receiver; there are 65535 available ports over which data can be sent on the Internet, some of them are dedicated to a specific, known purpose (such as 80 for http traffic, 443 for https traffic, 25 for SMTP traffic)

Primary Address Pool

The initial allocation of all available IP addresses which could be distributed to users around the world for use with websites and Internet-connected devices.

Query String Parameters

The last part of a URL following the domain name and resource information, it is prefixed by a question mark (?)

Retry Interval

Used by mail servers to indicate how long it will wait between delivery attempts of an e-mail message. Most mail servers will have a number of retry intervals that increase in length from a few minutes initially to a few days at the end.

Reverse DNS

Used by e-mail servers (amongst others) to definitively tie an IP address to a domain name rather than the user DNS function which is the inverse of that

Router

Hardware device on a network used to determine where to send data packets

Routing table

List of known destinations that is stored by a router, it will link IP addresses (or groups) to an interface.

SMTP (Simple Mail Transfer (or Transport) Protocol)

An e-mail protocol used specifically for the sending of e-mails as opposed to retrieving them which is dealt with by IMAP or POP

Sender Policy Framework (SPF)

A DNS initiative to limit the IP Addresses that can send e-mail for a given domain; this is used in an attempt to cut down on SPAM that is sent. Receiving e-mail servers will consult an SPF record to determine (in part) whether or not to accept an e-mail for delivery

Soft Bounce

A report to a sending party that the e-mail message they have sent could not be delivered, but the reason for non-delivery is not permanent, and may well be resolved given time. An example would be that the receiving mailbox is over its storage limit

Start of Authority (SOA)

Important summary information about a domain that is contained in the DNS record

Static content

Website page content that is stored in a file, and displayed identically to each visitor when requested. Opposite of dynamic content (see above).

Sub-domain

Sub-division mechanism for a domain name, shown to the left of a domain name in the URL, domains can have an unlimited number of sub-domains, so too each sub-domain can have an unlimited number of sub-domains.

Three Tier Architecture

Description of a method of designing a website or application. So called as the three concerns of that application are separated from each other. Those tiers (concerns) are:

A. Back end (database)
B. Business logic
C. User Interface (the screens that your users interact with, like a web page for example)

Top level domain

The last part of a domain name, usually assigned to a country or region, or used as an organisational group. For example, .com or .fr and so on

URL (Universal Resource Locator)

The full path shown in the address bar of your web browser that points to a given resource (for example an image or a video) rather than a website or domain as a whole

Web browser

Software used on a computer or other device that is capable of navigating to and display the contents of a website

About the author

Initially from London, England, I have worked in a number of countries around the world before settling in Australia – Adelaide to be precise if you hadn't spotted the subtle references throughout the book - to continue with the IT career which I got into twenty odd years ago, after trying a few others out for size to start with.

I started writing code when I was about seven years old, although that was entirely from weekly magazines with program listings that my granddad bought for me without fail each and every time they were made available at the newsagent; I guess he, like my parents, knew that computers would be my life and that was over thirty years ago. To be fair, I wasn't doing IT professionally at age seven or so, that came a little later but computers have been part of my life that entire time: from spending days as a teenager convincing a dot matrix printer to play nicely with a Commodore Amiga, to my first professional application – which happened to be for a division of the Financial Times – there has always been a computer around.

With their continued presence in the world, it always seemed a bit strange that people didn't like these things that I used all the time, they were scared of them. I guess that's what a learning barrier and a whole bunch of jargon will do to an industry. To be honest, the worst thing that happened to the computer industry is techies; the book talks about the stereotypical IT guy a bit, but they don't define us all: we're not all like that. Some of us even come out in daylight and are able to talk to people. Sometimes.

The writing of a book came completely out of left field; I don't even read for pleasure, only for reference. So the non-reader suddenly becomes the writer, bizarre. This book was never meant to be a book, it was meant to be a video-based lecture series, but as I was writing the notes and the script for that series, it kind of just became more like a book than a video. It was only a few changes from one format to the other – mostly a search/replace for the words "course" and "book" as it happens.

And that's why the book is written like it is, this is the way that I speak; everyone who has read the draft text has said that they have read the text in my voice because it is just almost identical. A massive thank you to Claire for her many hours with the red pen over the drafts, and to Rob for "glancing at it while he was making a cup of tea", they both helped heaps.

So that's me, the London lad who started out as a travel agent, and still having read only a handful of books in his entire life, now on the other side of the world, having written one to teach you guys all about IT.

For part of my day job I help people exactly like you, people who call the company I work at, looking for help or advice. People who quite often have no idea what they need help with, all they know is that they have been left in the lurch by the IT guy who has up and left, now they have to fix it. Those people are almost exclusively owners and managers of small companies, and with a little bit of pointing in the right direction they are able to rebuild their world. You get the same help now without having to be in the same predicament that those callers find themselves in, but by the same token, you also don't get to hear the voice that people have read the book used. Ah well, that's life I guess.

Will there be more books? I don't know. At the moment there are no plans for any, but there wasn't a plan for this one and now look what's happened.

Whenever the next thing comes up that was going to be a video until the script went the other way, I'll maybe have a go at it, but until then, I'll just continue doing what I do; building the software and websites that I build and bouncing around the world a bit. We'll see.

Until next time, or maybe not.

Cheers

Mike

Made in United States
Orlando, FL
04 November 2026

90207819R00075